INDEX ON CENSORSHIP 2 1999

INDEX

Volume 28 No 2 March/April 1999 Issue 187

WEBSITE NEWS UPDATED EVERY TWO WEEKS

www.indexoncensorship.org
contact@indexoncensorship.org
tel: 0171-278 2313
fax: 0171-278 1878

Index on Censorship (ISSN 0306-4220) is published bi-monthly by a non-profit-making company: Writers & Scholars International Ltd, Lancaster House, 33 Islington High Street, London N1 9LH. *Index on Censorship* is associated with Writers & Scholars Educational Trust, registered charity number 325003 *Periodicals postage*: (US subscribers only) paid at Newark, New Jersey. Postmaster: send US address changes to *Index on Censorship* c/o Mercury Airfreight International Ltd Inc, 365 Blair Road, Avenel, NJ 07001, USA
© This selection Writers & Scholars International Ltd, London 1999
© Contributors to this issue, except where otherwise indicated

Subscriptions (6 issues per annum)
Individuals: UK £39, US $52, rest of world £45
Institutions: UK £44, US $80, rest of world £50
Speak to Tony Callaghan on 0171 278 2313

Index **thanks the Norwegian Royal Ministry of Foreign Affairs for their generous support. Thanks too to Mette Newth and the Norwegian Forum for Freedom of Expression**

EDITORIAL

Shelf life

'It is the most democratic of institutions because no one – but no one at all – can tell you what to read and when and how'. So writes Doris Lessing about the library, an institution which many of us take for granted – though Alberto Manguel wonders whether library democracy is not somewhat illusory. They are only two of the many distinguished contributors to this issue of *Index*, which celebrates the reopening this year of the Library of Alexandria, once the great symbol of the ancient world.

Nadine Gordimer remembers censored libraries in South Africa under apartheid; Sonallah Ibrahim recalls the secret building up of his prison library; Doris Lessing describes people's yearning in book-starved Zimbabwe; Michael Holroyd tells us how he owes his education to Maidenhead Public Library; Ivan Klíma reminds us of the absurdities of censoring bureaucracies, Wole Soyinka of the subversive power of words, Ted Hughes of books as memory – 'Decay of libraries is like/Alzheimer's in the nation's brain'.

We include a passionate account of what learning to read means for adult literacy students in Britain. Ever since the Free Library movement of the nineteenth century, libraries have been a focal point for British cultural life. But our present record is depressing. Many students now have to pay to use university libraries. Ten times more people go to libraries than to league football matches, yet local authorities are closing scores of them down – 22 in the London borough of Lambeth alone; though the government has recently shown signs of putting libraries higher up the political agenda.

Less reassuring is the government's latest Immigration and Asylum Bill, the toughest attempt yet to limit the number of refugees coming to Britain. Asylum seekers will have no choice about where they live, cash benefits are to be replaced by vouchers (on the grounds that cash payments are an incentive for 'economic' migrants; there is absolutely no evidence for this), and those who go to judicial review while their case is being considered will lose all support.

Meanwhile, Gerhard Schröder's recent proposal for dual citizenship for Germany's immigrants was followed by a huge electoral backlash against his Party. Yet, as the EC Social Affairs Commissioner reminded us, 'immigration has been a positive process which has brought economic and cultural benefits both to the host countries and to the immigrants themselves'. The growing anti-immigration bias in European social and political discourse can only strengthen racism and make more possible a grim Fortress Europe, inward looking and closed. ❏

contents

Everyday cruelty in Nazi Germany: the secret archives

p73

The new journalism in Moscow, Kiev and Minsk

p180

5	**EDITORIAL Ursula Owen**
8	**IN THE NEWS**
	NEWS ANALYSIS
15	**UK Tony Geraghty** A trip into Blair's labyrinth
19	**UK John O'Farrell** The unforgiven
21	**ZIMBABWE Regina Jere-Malanda** Mugabe hits out
	OPINION
24	**Gara LaMarche** The price of hate
28	**WORD POWER**
30	**Ted Hughes** Hear It Again
32	**Alberto Manguel** Libraries and their ashes
39	**Ivan Klima** A benefactor of the library
46	**Luciano Canfora** The vanished library
54	**Andrew Hammond** Echoes of lost grandeur
59	**Sonallah Ibrahim** There's no beating that devil
66	**Martín Espada** Prisoner AM-8335 and his Library of Lions
68	**Ahdaf Soueif** Cry havoc
73	**Peter Morgan** Bureaucracy of evil
77	**Michael Walsh** The splendour of truth
81	**Iaguba Diallo** Suddenly last summer
84	**Nadine Gordimer** Morning in the library: 1975
88	**Michael Foley** Marsh's Library
91	**John Medcalf** Barefoot messengers
94	**Wole Soyinka** Two Poems for the Pen
98	**FLASHPOINTS** Sierra Leone
100	**INDEX INDEX**
128	**PHOTOSTORY Melanie Friend** Kosovo: home and away
	WORD POWER II
134	**Susan Whitfield** In praise of the plagiarist
139	**Michael Holroyd** Places of opportunity
144	Library records
147	**Maria Margaronis** Purgation and liberation
152	**Jasmina Tesanovic** Secrets and lies
158	**Doris Lessing** Books for the hungry
160	**Anon** The adventures of Mr X
164	Embattled books
166	Lost libraries of the twentieth century
168	**POETRY Yang Lian** The sea stands still
170	**BABEL Emily Mitchell** Strangers in a strange land
175	**NEW MEDIA Arthur C Clarke** Orbital libraries
180	**DIARY Michael Foley** A tale of three cities
186	**MUSIC Arif Azad** Musical obsession
191	**LETTER Brian McGee** Cuba: a skewed utopia

● **In the beginning was the pixel** The ultra-orthodox Jews of Israel have sorted out what to do with the word 'God' on screen. Matter printed with the word *elohim* must be 'stored', or ritually buried under Jewish law. Rabbi Moshe Shaul Klein judges the word is simply an assemblage of pixels. 'It's not like you're throwing away anything more than a sequence of ones and zeroes'.

● **Hands up for haloes** A World Bank report, leaked to the *New York Times*, reveals that the institution knew all along of Indonesia's economic weakness, but said nothing for fear of threatening its image as a 'growth promoter'. Indonesia consumed US$25 billion of Bank funding during ex-president Suharto's 33-year rule, creating a 'halo effect', which, according to managers, prevented them from delivering tougher messages.

● **Truth-in-slaughtering** Beverly Hills could become the first US city to require furriers to add tags informing buyers of how their stoles were acquired. If approved in a May referendum, the labels will read: 'This product is made from animals that may have been killed by electrocution, gassing, neck-breaking, poisoning, clubbing, stomping or drowning and they may have been trapped in steel-jaw leg hold traps.'

● **To coin a phrase** In the backwash of the Euro's launch, the French Academy has officially advised against using the Orwellian term 'Euroland', preferring to describe the nations sharing the currency as 'Euro Zone'. The Academy is alarmed about further Anglo-Saxon linguistic encroachments, though the British have signed up neither to Land nor Zone.

● **Policing accountancy** Washington mayor Anthony Williams announced in February he will re-hire David Howard, who resigned after a black employee complained of his using the word 'niggardly' in reference to a tight budget. The mayor acknowledged he had 'acted too hastily', but the cleaning supervisor is seeking legal advice on the phrase 'spic and span'.

● **Silver service** The sixth annual ceremony of the Golden Lens, organised by the Turkish Association of Magazine Journalists, erupted when Kurdish singer Ahmet Kaya announced that his next *chanson* would be in Kurdish. Leading personalities from the Turkish music and film world hurled their knives and forks at the singer, who had to be escorted home by police.

● **Time travel** A missing *Dr Who* episode, which *afficionados* feared had been wiped, has surfaced at a collectors fair in New Zealand. Entitled *The Lion* and set in the Crusades, the Doctor (William Hartnell) battles with Islamic warriors instead of his customary enemy, the Daleks. But the BBC in 1969 worried that the episode might offend Muslims and banned distribution in Arabic-speaking countries. Thirty years on, the censored tape has been hailed as a classic and is due to be released as a special collectors' edition.

● **Shot from both sides** Walt Disney seems to have lost the gift for predicting market response. Its cartoon *Mulan*, about a Chinese girl who dresses as a man to replace her father in battle, has been condemned by Turkey's neo-fascist Nationalist Action Party (MHP) 'for showing the Huns as bad and the Chinese as peaceful'. MHP's vice-president said the film did more harm than *Midnight Express*, which told the story of an American drug-smuggler in a Turkish prison. Peaceful China isn't too happy either, although *Mulan* was finally granted permission to screen in

Shanghai for a month, after one year of waiting.

● **Old-time family values** Spain's public TV channel has withdrawn a drama about King Philip II because 'it made more sense to combine it with a series on his father'. The programme highlighted Philip's anti-semitism and his role in the Inquisition, which the Spanish State Memorial Society for the Philip II and Charles V Anniversaries rejects. The society has 'issued guidelines' that Philip be portrayed as a strictly 'morals and family' man. Academics were disturbed by what was seen as 'an attempt to brush up the darkest sides of a ruler who also preferred the brute suppression of dissidents to diplomacy'.

● **Eagle 1, Snake 1** Mexico's interior ministry banned the soccer team from wearing their new kit in a friendly with Argentina in February, because it featured the coat of arms that appears on the Mexican flag – an eagle clutching a snake. Official Jesus Reyna Garcia said he took the step because of a 'clear tendency toward commercial exploitation' and the National Anthem Law which forbids profiting from 'patriotic symbols'.

● **Dixie dissed** Texan high school principal George Cooper pulled a student editorial by Adam Martinez opposing the waving of the Confederate flag at a football game. Cooper said he censored it to avoid 'disrupting the school'. Trustees of Midland Independent High School voted to stop using the Rebel flag as a school symbol in 1991, although the football team is known as the Rebels and the student newspaper is called the *Dixie Dispatch*.

● **Bring back parrots** Furby, a furry cyberpet with owl features, has been banned from the National Security Agency in Maryland. Furby comes equipped with a chip that allows him to repeat what he has heard. Although his memory is limited to 100 English words and 100 in 'Furbish', anyone who brought the toy to work has been ordered to contact a security officer.

● **Nowhere to run** The capture of PKK leader Abdullah Ocalan exposed the West's long betrayal of Turkey's Kurds, for years the object of ethnic cleansing, as well as the murky operations of assorted spymasters in the eastern Mediterranean. More surprisingly, it revealed the strength of the organisation of the Kurdish diaspora in Europe, as protesters from Stockholm to Milan seized embassies and the media's attention.

Ocalan's flight from Syria to Russia to Italy and eventually to Greece confirmed that there is no place to hide from Washington's New World Order. No European country was able to withstand pressure from Turkey and the US for Ocalan's extradition, though Italy tried through legal means and Greece through clandestine ones. So far, no European body has moved to put pressure on Turkey for a fair and open trial, or to call for a peace conference between Turkey and the various Kurdish parties.

Turkey's role as a military outpost for the US among the oil fields of the Middle East is well known; its blossoming friendship with Israel cements a three-way alliance. A proposed oil pipeline from the Caucasus through Turkey, described as 'a centrepiece of American foreign policy,' adds urgency to the Kurdish 'problem'- an urgency Turkey underlined this February through a diplomatic flirtation with Iraq. Ocalan's head on a plate seems to have been, in part, a reassuring token to Ankara from its US patrons.

The Kurds at first turned their anger on the Greeks – if not quite their friends, at least their enemy's enemy. We may never know the details of what one Greek newspaper called 'The Ocalan Thriller,' but the drama that led to the PKK leader's capture combined geo-political pressures with atavistic domestic intrigue. The ultra-nationalist retired rear admiral who flew Ocalan into Greece had close ties to the Greek secret service which, to the government's embarrassment, was revealed as a surviving outpost of the old 'parastate' that has dogged efforts at democracy.

His action found an echo in Greek nationalism, on the rise since the break-up of Yugoslavia. From well-heeled Athenian matrons to salt-of-the-earth radicals, Greeks see Ocalan not only as the champion of an oppressed minority, but as a hero of the last liberation struggle against the Turks. Faced with the choice of turning Ocalan in – and provoking cries of treachery – or sheltering him – and risking war – the government chose a bungled mission to spirit him away. The crude pressure brought to bear by Washington can only have been an added incentive.

Ocalan is no Gandhi. The PKK,

an old-fashioned 'Stalinoid' organisation, has responded in kind to Turkish atrocities and turned brutally on suspected 'collaborators'. But we now know he is at least a symbolic leader for thousands of Kurds in Turkey and the diaspora. His arrest could be an opportunity for Turkey to work towards a political solution in Kurdistan. It is up to Europe to press it to do so.
Maria Margaronis

● **Squeezing the imagination**
Samia Mehrez, Professor of Modern Arabic Literature at the American University in Cairo (AUC), has come under attack for assigning her class the fictional autobiography of the Moroccan writer Muhammad Choukri, *Al-Khubz Al-Hafi*, translated by Paul Bowles as *For Bread Alone*.

Several students are believed to have complained about the 'pornographic' content of the novel to their parents, who brought it to the attention of the university physician who, in turn, alerted John Gerhart, President of the AUC. On 17 December, Professor Mehrez was whisked out of class to a meeting with the president, the provost, the dean and the physician. She was informed of the charge against her and of the university's desire that she withdraw the book and apologise to her class for assigning it. Mehrez, a

highly respected scholar, declined to do either, but expressed willingness to exclude the novel from the forthcoming exam.

A public campaign was subsequently launched by the newspapers *Al-Wafd* and *Al-Ahram Weekly* to discredit Professor Mehrez and embarrass the AUC. An immediate consequence was the removal from the campus bookstore of works deemed 'injurious to good taste', among them Sonallah Ibrahim's *The Smell of It* and Alifa Rifaat's *Distant View of a Minaret*. The curriculum committee was also reportedly considering removing al-Tayyib Salih's novel, *Season of Migration to the North*, from its reading list. In January, the campaign against Professor Mehrez grew steadily more vicious. She was charged with sexual harassment for assigning 'pornographic material' to 'minors' and 'forcing' them to discuss it.
**Magda Al-Nowaihi &
Muhammad Siddiq**

● **No speech for the wicked?**
On 2 February a federal jury in Oregon ordered two anti-abortion groups – the American Coalition of Life Advocates and the Portland-based Advocates for Life Ministries – to pay a US$107 million fine for displaying 'wanted' posters of 'baby butchers' on the Nuremberg Files website.

www.christiangallery.com/atrocity/
contains a directory of hundreds of
abortionists, along with their
addresses, registration numbers and
children's names. The names of four
doctors and two clinicians, murdered
by activists, have been crossed off like
items on a grocery list. Since the
judgement, the site has been dropped
by its host server.

The class action suit was filed in
1995 by Planned Parenthood, the
Portland Feminist Women's Health
Center and five doctors, who claimed
the site violated the 1994 Clinic
Entrances Act, which has so far been
used only against people who bomb
clinics or attack doctors. The
American Civil Liberties Union has
been divided on the case: in 1995, it
declined to defend the activists on
the grounds that the 'First
Amendment cannot be used as a
shield for individuals who engage in
violent acts', but it also fears the
implications of the views of the anti-
abortionists being interpreted as
incitement to violence, rather than as
free expression.

The federal decision will almost
certainly be referred to the US
Supreme Court. The site has since
been mirrored by Karin Spaink, a
Dutch columnist and Internet free
speech advocate and can be found at
*www.xs4all.nl/~kspaink/nuremberg/inde
x.html* **Latest:** In response to what
she calls 'heated debate' Karin has

removed the mirrored site and posted
an article explaining her position at
*www.xs4all.nl/~kspaink/nuremberg/abor
ts.html* More on this debate next
issue. **Billie Felix Jeyes**

● **Who's stalking Joe?** The
premises of Live FM, the radio
station belonging to the outspoken
former Labour Party minister Joe
Grima, was destroyed by fire on 24
January, highlighting the holiday
island of Malta as a new censorship
hotspot. Grima, who also presents
the programme *Protagonisti* on the
Nationalist Party's Net TV, has been
the victim of three arson attacks since
last November when his car was set
ablaze. Subsequently, intruders set
alight a room in Live FM and fire also
gutted his villa at Zejtun. 'What has
been done to me,' Grima said after
the most recent attack, 'is just abject
hatred and jealousy. I am still a
protagonist, in spite of the fact that I
have left politics.' Grima's
transformation from Labour stalwart
to an ebullient presenter at Net TV is
viewed as both a defection by his
former associates and an incursion by
his erstwhile rivals. 'If Mr Grima is
muzzled,' wrote Simone Zammit
Endrich in the local *Times*, '... the
voice of truth would most likely start
to erode gradually.' ❏
Michael Griffin

TONY GERAGHTY

A trip into Blair's labyrinth

Despite movement towards peace, army activities in Northern Ireland remain a dangerous subject for any British writer

More than 20 years ago I was discussing political manipulation, censorship and sexuality with the novelist James Baldwin. Baldwin – former Harlem preacher and *New York Times* reporter covering the first of Martin Luther King's marches – wore a fetching caftan. He was attended by acolytes, living as a left-handed, homosexual, black American, socialist exile in Provence. He intoned, in Bible-reading rhythms: 'Listen! If they got you watchin' that thing danglin' 'tween your legs, they don't need no CIA to watch you. And why is that you ask? Because you – You! – is watchin' yourself!' His cascading laughter was a shrill, mocking message that no words of mine could capture.

I have thought much of that conversation lately, since 6.50am on 3 December to be precise: the moment when six detectives from the Ministry of Defence Police knocked on the door of my seventeenth century cottage, in reassuring, rustic Herefordshire, and arrested me. Censorship, I was about to learn, was more than a concept of abstract concern to – as Alastair Campbell would put it – 'middle class wankers'. It is a physical and psychological experience that leaves the victim feeling that he has contracted a political version of AIDs, a sense that his privacy was illusory; an awareness that nothing committed to paper or computer or spoken within earshot of a microphone, in or out of the police interrogation room, is safe. The surveillance apparatus of the state marks home and hearth with an odour of fascism that no amount of liberal discussion can deodorise or exorcise. What is lost is the sense of self-possession itself, the very belief in freedom.

Was my name Geraghty? Had I written a book entitled *The Irish War?* Yes and yes again. I am a recidivist among writers, at it as journalist and author since I left school, aged 16, on 18 December 1948. The eerily polite MoD team, five men and one athletic woman to keep an eye on my even more athletic wife, spent the next seven hours and 30 minutes searching a home crammed with files and books. At about 2.30pm they left with my computer, modem, many files... and myself, in an unmarked car. It was not unlike a day in Nigeria in 1968, during the Biafran War, when four other polite men, their ritual scars identifying them as Yoruba, put me into an anonymous Mini for a long drive to captivity in Lagos. The only difference, this time, was that I, the prisoner, had to direct my captors to the local police station. There, the local station sergeant had trouble choosing the appropriate computer heading for my case. 'We don't get many official secrets cases in Leominster,' he explained.

I spent the next five hours in custody for two sessions of questioning about pages in my book describing how computerised surveillance systems, necessarily evolved for an exotic war across the water, are now being deployed against civilians in mainland Britain. In particular, the MoD men wanted to know about my sources and were clearly irritated when I spoke about the 'sanctity' of such things, even when they are gift-wrapped by the Downing Street lobby system. Another, similar session followed on 29 January, at which point the matter was passed to the Crown Prosecution Service. The CPS, advised by the Attorney-General, will have to decide whether I am to be the first writer to be prosecuted under Section 5 of the Official Secrets Act 1989, that part of the censorship law specifically aimed at scribes. The maximum sentence, on conviction, is two years.

In view of the release rate of convicted terrorist murderers and other political psychopaths, I doubt whether I shall have the chance to compare notes with any of them if I go down later this year. Meanwhile my book, the source of the trouble, a hypothetical threat to national security, continues to be sold freely throughout the realm.

Whatever the outcome I am surprised, as a battle-hardened old fossil, to be scarred by the censorship experience so far. Before the raid I had had intimations that something nasty was about to happen but I disregarded most of them, not wishing to surrender to paranoia. This, after all, was Britain 1998, not 1940, not Britain with her back to the wall, the blitzed London of my childhood and with that, the experience of being buried under a building demolished by a flying bomb. This was also Blair's Brave New Britain. As for those Irish Republicans and their families, well of course they were asking for it. I had even made a neat, cerebral comparison in my book between the crude resettlement of hundreds of thousands of civilians into fortified villages in Malaya, necessary to win that war 40 years ago, with its modern equivalent: a selective, invisible, electronic cage that is thrown around neighbourhoods, families and individuals, thanks to systems with such engaging code-names as 'Glutton'. But this was not the stuff of real life in the hamlet of Hope-Under-Dinmore where I had chosen to put down some roots, at last. Or so I thought.

The raid went through the dirty linen basket and the erotica, some of it collected for a novel which links themes from ancient mythology – bestiality and incest – with modern practice. The team were careful and systematic. One did the scale drawings, showing the layout of each room as it was searched. Another, donnish figure claimed to be the computer expert. Two more went for the documentary evidence.

A fifth man – sweating unnaturally most of the time – claimed he was the photographer but was clearly incapable of attaching a wide-angled lens to the camera with which he seemed strangely unfamiliar. I was reminded of an account of infantry soldiers searching homes in Northern Ireland, dressed in their camouflaged 'cabbage suits', accompanied by a suitably disguised technician from MI5, whose job it was to plant the bugs.

The subjects of that search, veterans by now, said to each soldier, 'Yuz are real "Angle Iron",' [Royal Anglian Regiment] 'but you,' – pointing accusingly at the odd man out, 'yuz is fucking MI5. Get out of here.'

The cost of an electronic sweep for hidden microphones – £1,200 – was more than I wished to pay at this point. Instead, my wife and I now take a walk whenever we wish to discuss sensitive issues; or sit in the bathroom with the taps running. We arrange for letters that we prefer are not exposed to government spies to be sent to a friend's address. Our neighbours, hearing of the raid, reacted like Frenchmen under Occupation and offered barns, outhouses and attics as places of further concealment, were that ever necessary. About two days after the raid, a hazard warning light flashed on the steering wheel of my Peugeot, indicating an airbag fault. I drove to my local garage and asked the chief mechanic – an old soldier who knows the score – to check the vehicle for hidden devices. My telephone conversations are, inevitably, cryptic and important discussions must now be face-to-face, far from any street.

Over-reaction? What *is* over-reaction? During my third interrogation session on 29 January it became apparent that the MoD Police (answerable to whom?) had accessed my credit card account for the preceding 13 months in order to determine on what day I had purchased a railway ticket for £27.05. The official effort invested in keeping watch on me was at a level appropriate to the sort of terrorist now being released from the Maze.

My real sin might have been to decline an invitation from a rear-admiral in Whitehall, secretary of the censorship machine once known as the D-Notice Committee, to show him part of my book before it was published. The admiral, though on MoD's payroll, with an office in MoD Main Building, serving a committee chaired by the permanent under secretary of that ministry, denies that he is answerable to MoD. In spite of that, I declined his invitation, since the censorship system that he runs, day to day, is notionally voluntary. Why was I so obstinate? After all, the vast majority of books on military affairs in this country *is* thoroughly censored, though the reader who buys them is never told that. (Should they carry a health warning?)

My experience does not instill confidence in their system. In 1992, the BBC 'Newsnight' reporter Mark Urban submitted his revealing account of the undercover war in Ireland – *Big Boys' Rules* – for censorship and he was betrayed. I know he was betrayed because an uncensored copy of the proof was passed to me in breach of the confidentiality Whitehall guarantees to those writers who collaborate with it. From the admiral's office, proofs are distributed to such agencies as MI5, ostensibly to be sanitised in the national interest. In practice, a mole-hunt begins to identify the author's sources.

When the MoD's detectives came upon Urban's proof they asked: 'Has this been published?' I said it had. I had in mind the book, not the naughty bits. They put it back on the shelf and passed on. I now feel obliged to hide it a long way from home, just in case. This is not quite a life on the run, but it has domestic parallels. I am now beginning – as James Baldwin said I would – to watch myself. Censorship is indeed a state of mind in which the mind is under siege. It is a process that occupies the sleeping as well as the waking state. It is a nightmare out of

the pages of George Orwell and a labyrinth in which the victim
encounters a minotaur partly of his own making. It is far from the
Freedom of Information that Blair and his Lord Chancellor keep
promising us. With luck, I might be in front of No 1 Court at the Old
Bailey at about the same time as the next Queen's Speech. At least the
enemy will then be tangible if no less real. ❏

Tony Geraghty is the author of The Irish War *(HarperCollins, 1998) ISBN:
0002556170*

JOHN O'FARRELL

The unforgiven

**Eamon Collins, the IRA man turned peace proponent, died
where he lived, erasing the word 'tout' from his walls while his
neighbours watched and waited**

Eamon Collins' last creative act was a piece of editing. On the day he
was murdered, he left his house early, before daybreak. Local IRA
supporters had painted hostile graffiti at the end of his street: 'Collins –
RUC TOUT'. 'Tout' is the local slang for police informer, a charge
Collins had always denied. Yes, he had cracked under interrogation by
the Royal Ulster Constabulary, he had named names he knew to be his
comrades in the IRA's South Armagh Brigade, but he hadn't taken
money, or fantasised about being a police secret agent.

He still called himself an Irish Republican. He reiterated that with
black paint on the morning he died. With thick black brushstrokes, he
excised his own name and one letter from the gable-end libel, changing
it to ' ★★★★★★★ RUC ★OUT'. That was his last public statement. Eamon
Collins is not an informer, but proud to be a republican.

It did not save him. He returned to his home in a totally nationalist
housing estate in Newry, County Down. Minutes later, two men called
at his door. He left the house with them in the pre-dawn light. At 6am,

he was found beaten beyond recognition and covered with stab wounds.

Eamon Collins was not a popular man. Journalists found him arrogant, yet many depended on his insights into IRA thinking. Many expressed astonishment that he continued to live in Newry in the midst of the South Armagh Brigade of the IRA. He had a messianic zeal when confronting men he knew to be still 'involved', trying to convince them that republican objectives could be reached without 'armed struggle'.

Yet despite his philosophy, which objectively mirrored the thinking of the Sinn Féin leadership and Gerry Adams in particular, he got no support from that quarter of the republican movement. As far as republicans were concerned, he broke his word to them several times. In 1985, he broke down after five days and nights of constant questioning and gave the RUC the names of over 50 people he claimed were active in the IRA in South Armagh. Although he retracted his evidence and always made the distinction between himself and 'touts' such as Seán O'Callaghan, he remained unforgiven.

In the early 1990s, he met in Belfast with a senior republican. He asked if he and his family could return to Newry and live unmolested. Yes, he was told, if he 'kept his head down'. He didn't. He made a television documentary in 1995 which outlined his career as an IRA Intelligence Officer. Unionist MPs, including David Trimble, raised the programme in the House of Commons, demanding his prosecution for offences he admitted in the programme, but for which he had earlier evaded justice.

His book *Killing Rage*, published by Granta in 1997, caused more storms of controversy, this time among republicans who objected to his portrayal of the 'struggle' as nasty, brutish and, occasionally, drunk. Ironically, on the day he was savagely killed by persons (as yet) unknown, the anti-Agreement unionist MP Jeffrey Donaldson tabled an early day motion in the House of Commons calling on the home secretary to protect the feelings of victims hurt by 'the manner in which terrorists are able to profit from their past crime' by publishing books. *Killing Rage* was not mentioned but Donaldson was prompted to raise this issue by a front page story in the previous day's *News Letter*, in which Paul Toombs, whose father Ivan was set up to be murdered by his customs and excise colleague Eamon Collins, called for such action. 'We feel we can no longer remain silent while Collins continues to make money off the back of our father's murder,' he said.

Collins was due to give evidence two weeks after the time of his death on behalf of the *Sunday Times* in an appeal brought by the newspaper against Patrick Murphy, who had successfully sued the paper in Dublin. Collins would have testified that the *Sunday Times* was correct to allege that Murphy was a Provo. Last year, Collins gave evidence for the same newspaper when Thomas 'Slab' Murphy lost his libel trial.

The *Sunday Times* paid Collin £10,000 for his expert testimony. Perhaps that money was viewed by the local IRA as evidence that Collins had finally gone the way of the 'tout'. But giving evidence against the local Provo *capo* alone could have been enough to seal his fate. But there were, in any case, others who hated Collins enough to bludgen him to death.

Collins also spoke out against the INLA and the Real IRA. He accused the former of being more interested in drug deals than 'national liberation', and the latter of being throwbacks to the vicious sectarian catholic nationalism which threatens catholics as much as protestants.

Who killed Eamon Collins? Take your pick. Was he killed for speaking out, or simply for questioning the sectarian shibboleths of rural republicanism, where the terms of the 'struggle' are comfortably painted in black and white, shades away from the multi-coloured, multicultural fudge of the Good Friday Agreement? That's anyone's guess. ❑

John O'Farrell is the editor of Fortnight

REGINA JERE-MALANDA

Mugabe hits out

Judges, journalists and elements of Zimbabwe's military join forces against their President, who, as usual, is far from amused

Never noted for a particularly robust press, the effectively one-party state of President Robert Mugabe displayed its contempt for the rule of law in January after the independent weekly *Standard* published a report that 23 soldiers had been detained for plotting to overthrow the government. *Standard* editor Mark Chavunduka and reporter Roy Choto were arrested by military police on 12 and 19 January, respectively, and charged under the Law and Order Maintenance Act, introduced by then Prime Minister Garfield Todd in 1960 to contain the emergent 'nationalist menace'. The act allows for seven-year sentences for 'false' stories deemed likely to cause 'fear, alarm or despondency among the public'.

Chavunduka had every reason to feel that despondency himself. During his incarceration at Cranborne Barrack near Harare, he was denied access to legal representation, medical assistance or the support of family and friends. On 14 January, the High Court ordered Defence Minister Moven Mahachi to release the editor, arguing that his detention was unlawful. Mahachi refused, claiming civilian courts had no jurisdiction over military camps such as the one where Chavunduka was being held.

Choto, the man who actually broke the coup story, was arrested one week later. On 21 January, when the two journalists were finally released on bail, they related how they had been beaten with fists, wooden planks and rubber sticks – particularly on the soles of their feet – and had received electric shocks to their genitals. They were also subjected to the 'submarine' torture, in which their heads were wrapped in plastic bags and submerged in a water tank.

Government paranoia over what the press did, or did not, know about the hypothetical coup spread like spilt petrol. A day earlier, on 20 January, a secret service officer stormed the offices of the weekly *Tribune*, the *Zimbabwe Monitor* and state-controlled Zimbabwe Information Service in the southern town of Masvingo, beating up four journalists, a guard and a member of the advertising staff. A day after the release of Chavunduka and Choto, the Criminal Investigation Department arrested *Standard* managing editor Clive Wilson and held him for three days until the Attorney General intervened by refusing to prosecute on the grounds of lack of evidence.

Later in the month, police used tear gas and batons to break up a protest march against the journalists' arrests by some 200 lawyers. 'I think our government has a siege mentality,' said Tendai Bitti of Lawyers for Human Rights. 'This government views the army as its personal property to be used against the people, and the law can go to hell.'

And not just the law. On 4 February, information minister Chen Mutengwende said that the current media environment was 'too relaxed and had allowed the penetration of media organisations with a political agenda to destroy the government and the country'. Breaking his own silence over the torture of the *Standard*'s journalists, President Mugabe warned the press that, unless 'their insidious acts of sabotage cease immediately, my government will be compelled to take very stern measures against ... white persons of British extraction and those they have elected to be their puppets'.

Mugabe accused three Supreme Court judges and one High Court judge of 'an outrageous and deliberate act of impudence' for speaking out against the illegal detention of the journalists. 'The judiciary has no right whatsoever to give instructions to the President on any matter, as the four judges have purported to do,' he said. 'We as a state cannot trust these judges any longer,' he continued. 'The one and only honourable course open to them is to quit the bench and join the political forum.' ❏

Regina Jere-Malanda is a freelance journalist from Zambia who has worked for Agence France Presse and as Africa Researcher for Index on Censorship.

APOLOGY: We very much regret the unfortunate error that resulted in our ascribing the article on Fela Kuti 'From praise to protest' (Smashed Hits 6th/99) to an unknown. The article was written by Rotimi Sankore, a Nigerian journalist currently based in the UK

GARA LAMARCHE

The price of hate

It's not safe to be gay in the USA. How to curb the most blatant and insidious form of late-twentieth century hate speech?

The murder rate has been declining throughout most of the United States over the last few years, but one killing this autumn shocked many Americans into outrage: the torture and beating of Wyoming college student Matthew Shepard, tied to a fence and left to die. As nearly everyone knows, this was not a random slaying, but a crime of hate. Shepard was marked for death because he was gay.

In the wake of this horrible act, there has been condemnation all round. Supporters of gay and lesbian rights have called for a stronger government response, including hate crimes legislation (Wyoming has none at all). Most opponents of gay rights have also denounced the violence and called for the punishment of those responsible. (A sniper's shooting, at around the same time, of Barnett Slepian, a Buffalo, NY doctor who performed abortions, raises similar issues and produced a similar response on both sides of the abortion debate.)

I believe that hate crime laws have a place, and see no reason why a killer who chooses his or her victims on the basis of their identity – such as race or sexual orientation – or, for that matter, on their exercise of a constitutionally protected right such as having or providing an abortion, should not pay a heavier price. We do it, for example, with the killers of police officers and various federal officials. But I have little faith that increased penalties will deter violent hate crimes. Because it is urgent that we find some means of doing so – for the murder of Matthew Shepard is the tip of an iceberg of daily assault and harassment suffered by gay people – I believe the time has come to do more. The time has come to curb hate speech.

I don't mean the kind of speech that employs vulgar and noxious racial or homophobic epithets, although its users should certainly be condemned and shunned, as, for the most part, they are. And I don't mean legal curbs, since I continue to believe that the First Amendment bars, as it should, criminal or other governmental sanctions for offensive expression.

I mean the most effective hate speech, effective because it never uses the forbidden words that isolate utterers from mainstream society, and because it comes from the mouths of those whose positions afford them both a wide audience and the cloak of credibility and authority. Here are some examples:

• Reverend Jerry Falwell: 'Homosexuality is moral perversion and is always wrong. God hates homosexuality.'

• Senator Jesse Helms: 'A lot of us are sick and tired of all the pretences of injured innocence. They are not innocent!'

• Reverend Pat Robertson: 'Homosexuality is an abomination. The practices of these people are appalling. It is a pathology. It is a sickness. Many of those people with Adolf Hitler were Satanists; many of them were homosexuals. The two things seem to go together.'

• Senate Majority Leader Trent Lott: Homosexuality is 'a sin'. 'You should try to show them a way to deal with that problem, just like alcohol ... or sex addiction ... or kleptomaniacs.'

The list could go on and on, including the South Carolina Republican Party spokesperson who told the *New York Times* that the party doesn't even have to poll its members' views on homosexuality, since 'it would be like asking everybody if they're for free ice cream', or the Greenville minister and organiser of Citizens for Traditional Family Values who calls homosexuality 'demonic' and 'a stench in the nostrils of God'.

The stench, it's plain, has a different source. Does anyone doubt that the hateful rhetoric of politicians and preachers, no doubt intended 'merely' to stoke a political and fundraising base, ends, too often, in blood? As Christine Quinn, executive director of the New York City Gay and Lesbian Anti-Violence Project, pointed out at the time of Senator Lott's remarks, his 'ridiculous and hateful' statements 'affirm Americans' homophobia and compel them to act that homophobia out in the form of violent acts against lesbian, gay, bisexual and transgender people.'

The Shepard murder reveals just how misguided has been the raucous

Jerry Falwell – Credit: Rex

debate over hate speech, which has roiled civil liberties and civil rights groups for the last 10 years. It's been focused on fine-tuning the civil rights and incitement laws, but even if successful (and no such laws have sustained court challenge) a tighter hate speech regimen would catch the little fish while the big ones swim through the net. And even those who are trying to come up with non-legal remedies – like the leaders of the Anti-Defamation League, who have just unveiled a new internet 'filter' to screen out hate speech – are missing the point. No filter would block a confused and unstable person from reading the words of Jesse Helms or Pat Robertson.

What's needed is a campaign for moral accountability aimed at those with power and influence: a concerted effort to isolate and shame those whose overheated rhetoric dehumanises lesbians and gay men, paving the way for others' violence.

Not so long ago, segregationist political leaders spoke of African-Americans in similar terms – with similar violent consequences, particularly in the south – to those used by today's homophobic senators and preachers. They don't do so today because it would carry unacceptable consequences. Any political or religious leader who spoke of blacks or Jews in the way that Senators Helms and Lott do about gays, would quickly be marginalised. He or she might find an audience at rallies or on the internet, but many other doors would be closed. Mainstream political figures would not want to share a podium with you; newspapers would not publish your opinion pieces; talk shows would not book you.

Until we find a way to impose a similar cost on the most dangerous hate speech of the late 1990s, it will remain unsafe to be gay. ❏

Gara LaMarche is director of US programmes for the Open Society Institute in New York, and editor of Speech and Equality: Do We Really Have to Choose? *(New York University Press, 1996)*

Credit: Erica Baum/D'Amelio Terras Gallery, New York

Word Power

The library has for centuries been the joy and refuge of those seeking knowledge. In celebration of the opening of the new Library of Alexandria later this year, *Index* looks at the library as liberator

TED HUGHES

Hear It Again

'For out of olde feldes, as men seyth,
Cometh al this newe corne yer by yere,
And out of olde bokes, in good feyth,
Cometh al this newe science that men lere.'

Chaucer: *The Parlement of Foules*

Fourteen centuries have learned,
From charred remains, that what took place
When Alexandria's library burned
Brain-damaged the human race.

Whatever escaped
Was hidden by bookish monks in their damp cells
Hunted by Alfred dug for by Charlemagne
Got through the Dark Ages little enough but enough
For Dante and Chaucer sitting up all night
looking for light.

A Serbian Prof's insanity,
Commanding guns, to split the heart,
His and his people's, tore apart
The Sarajevo library.

Tyrants know where to aim
As Hitler poured his petrol and tossed matches
Stalin collected the bards...
In other words the mobile and only libraries...
of all those enslaved peoples from the Black to
the Bering Sea
And made a bonfire
Of the mainsprings of national identities to melt
the folk into one puddle

And the three seconds of the present moment
By massacring those wordy fellows whose memories were
bigger than armies.

Where any nation starts awake
Books are the memory. And it's plain
Decay of libraries is like
Alzheimer's in the nation's brain.

And in my own day in my own land
I have heard the fiery whisper: 'We are here
To destroy the Book
To destroy the rooted stock of the Book and
The Book's perennial vintage, destroy it
Not with a hammer not with a sickle
And not exactly according to Mao who also
Drained the skull of adult and adolescent
To build a shining new society
With the empties...'

For this one's dreams and that one's acts,
For all who've failed or aged beyond
The reach of teachers here are found
The inspiration and the facts.

As we all know and have heard all our lives
Just as we've heard that here.

Even the most misfitting child
Who's chanced upon the library's worth,
Sits with the genius of the Earth
And turns the key to the whole world.

Hear it again. ❏

©*Ted Hughes*, *July 1997*
By kind permission of the Library and Information Comission. Reprinted from
New Library: The People's Network.

ALBERTO MANGUEL

Libraries and their ashes

No library is perfect – yet their exclusions, ommisions, classifications and obfuscations reveal just as much about their creator's intentions as do their contents

I remember, with a feeling of both fondness and apprehension, the libraries of my school days. I especially remember the library of the Colegio Nacional de Buenos Aires, my *alma mater*: the imposing wooden doors, the welcoming gloom, the green-shaded lamps that reminded me vaguely of the lamps in sleeping car compartments, the seemingly endless shelves of books towering up to the darkened ceiling, many of their pages undisturbed for decades. I remember the silence constantly broken by whispered snatches of conversation and nervous laughter, the distrustful librarian who was always trying to find excuses not to release the requested title, the forbidden sections at which certain books would spontaneously fall open: Lorca's poems at '*The Unfaithful Bride*', *La Celestina* at the brothel scene, Cortázar's *Los Premios* at the chapter in which the young boy is seduced by the sailor. How these fiery texts had found their way into our scrupulous library we never knew, and we wondered how long it would be before the librarian discovered that, under his very nose, generation after generation of corruptible students passed on to one another the names of secretly scandalous books.

Like that long-ago school library, every library contains texts that escape the librarians' vigilance and are secretly subversive, because subversiveness, much like proverbial beauty, lies in the eye of the beholder. As a child of seven, St Teresa of Avila read novels of chivalry in her father's library and they prompted her to defy her family, run away from home and (though she was found and sent back after barely a mile) 'seek martyrdom among the infidels in the land of the Moors'. As a prisoner in a Siberian labour camp, Joseph Brodsky read Auden's poems and they strengthened his resolve to defy his jailers and survive for the sake of a glimpsed-at freedom. Equally, those who take upon themselves the task of guarding the entrance to the library's stacks find danger where others will see none. General Pinochet famously banned *Don Quixote* from the libraries of Chile because he read in that novel an argument for civil disobedience, and the Japanese Minister of Culture, several years ago, objected to *Pinocchio* because it showed unflattering pictures of handicapped people in the figures of the cat who pretends to be blind and the fox who pretends to be lame. Equally intimate reasons have been given for banning everything, from *The Wizard of Oz* (a hotbed of pagan beliefs) to *The Catcher in the Rye* (a dangerous adolescent role model). In the words of William Blake:

> Both read the Bible day and night,
> But thou read'st black where I read white.

Legend has it that when the conqueror Amr ibn al-As entered Alexandria in 642, he ordered Caliph Umar I to set fire to the library's books. The story has been discredited, but Umar's apocryphal response deserves to be quoted because it echoes the curious logic of every book-burner then and now. Umar acquiesced by saying: 'If the contents of these books agree with the Holy Book, then they are redundant. If it disagrees, then they are undesirable. In either case, they should be consigned to the flames.' Umar was addressing, somewhat stridently it is true, the essential fluidity of literature. Because of it, no library is what it is set up to be. Even within the strictest circumscriptions, any choice of books will be vaster than its label and an inquiring reader will find danger (salutary or reprehensible) in the safest, most invigilated places.

Our mistake, perhaps, has been to look upon a library as an all-encompassing and neutral space. Any library is, by definition, the result of a choice, necessarily limited in its scope. The earliest Mesopotamian libraries we know of, leading back to the third millennium BC, were born under these conditions. Unlike official archives, set up to preserve the daily transactions and ephemeral dealings of a particular group, these primitive libraries collected works of a more general appeal, such as the so-called 'royal inscriptions', commemorative tablets of stone or metal that retold important political events. These libraries were, in all probability, privately owned, set up by lovers of the written word who would often instruct the scribes to copy the owner's name on the tablets, thereby marking the collection as the property of one man. Even when these libraries were attached to a temple, they usually carried the name of a high priest or some other important personage responsible for the collection. Already the early librarians were aware of how a particular shelving or cataloguing lends a book a particular sense, and some library books carried a warning colophon, intended to dissuade anyone wishing to tamper with the allotted category to which a book was destined by the owner. A dictionary from the seventh century BC concludes with this prayer: 'May Ishtar bless the reader who will not alter this tablet nor place it elsewhere in the library, and may She denounce in anger he who dares withdraw it from the building.'

Kings too set up libraries in their palaces. The most famous of these is the Library of Asurbanipal in Nineveh, founded c640 BC. This scholar-king, who copied and revised some of the books himself, sent orders to representatives throughout his kingdom to search for whatever volumes he felt his library was missing. We have a letter in which Asurbanipal, after listing the books he is seeking, insists that the task should be carried out without delay. 'Find them and send them to me. Nothing should detain them. And, in the future, if you discover other tablets not herewith mentioned, inspect them and, if you consider them of interest for the library, collect them and send them on to me.' Chance, as well as choice, shapes a library's catalogue.

Particulars of taste and idiosyncratic restrictions are to be expected in a private collection, but they inform as well libraries intended for a wider audience. A public library is a paradox, a building set aside for an essentially private craft (reading) which now must take place it in a communal space. Locked inside the realm of an individual book, each reader also forms part of the community of readers which the library defines. Under the library's roof, these readers share an illusion of freedom, convinced that the entire reading realm is theirs for the asking. In fact their choice is censored in a number of ways: by the stack (open or closed) on which the book sits, by the section of the library in which it has been catalogued, by privileged notions of reserved rooms or special collections, by generations of librarians whose ethics and tastes have shaped the collection, by official guidelines based on what society considers 'proper', by bureaucratic rulings whose *raison d'être* is lost in the dungeons of time, by considerations of budget and size and availability.

Under such conditions, the reader's duty is clearly to undermine these restrictions: to strip the book of its labels, to recognise the categories to which it has been condemned, to question the definition of a certain book by reading (as the phrase goes) 'between the lines'.

Even without reading between the lines of library books, any library, by its very existence, conjures up its forbidden or forgotten shadow: a concurrent and certainly greater library of the books that have not been included, those that for conventional reasons of quality, subject matter or even volume have been deemed unfit for survival under one specific roof. (I mention volume because this was the reason given for expurgating the new San Francisco Library. After completion, the architects realised that their building had even less shelving capacity than the one it was meant to replace; the director of the library therefore decided to eliminate any book that had not been taken out in the past five or six years, and since the municipal laws did not allow him to give away or sell the books, he ordered that they be pulped. To save the books, heroic employees stole into the library at night and stamped them with recent dates to save them from destruction. Unfortunately, a large number of books did not escape the purge; reduced to landfill, they form now one of those ghostly libraries of shadows, a memorial to one man's bureaucratic folly.)

These invisible and yet present libraries are formidable. The pagan authors banished from the early Christian libraries, the Arab and Jewish works excluded from the libraries of Spain after the expulsion, the 'degenerate' books condemned to the pyre by the Nazis, the 'bourgeois' writers proscribed by Stalin, the 'Communist scribblers' exiled by Senator McCarthy, all these constituted in their time colossal libraries waiting to be summoned by their future readers. After the notorious tyrant Mansur ibn Abi Amir, who died in 1002, condemned to the flames an important collection of scientific and philosophical works assembled in the Andalusian libraries by his predecessors, the historian Saïd the Spaniard was moved to observe: 'These sciences were despised by the old and criticised by the mighty, and the men who studied them were accused of heresy and heterodoxy. Thereafter, those who had the knowledge held their tongue, went into hiding and kept secret what they knew, in trust for a more enlightened age.'

Sometimes, of course, exclusion is not enough. Existing libraries, in their very being, seem to question the authority of those in power. As repositories of history or sources for the future, as guides or manuals for difficult times, as symbols of authority past or present, the books in a library stand for more than their collective contents and have, since the beginning of the written word, been threatened with destruction. It hardly matters why a library is destroyed: every banning, curtailment, destruction, plundering or looting immediately gives rise to a louder, braver, more durable library composed of the banned, looted, plundered, destroyed or curtailed books. They may no longer be available for consultation, they may only exist in the vague memory of a reader or in the vaguer still memory of tradition and legend, but they will have acquired a kind of immortality through censorship intentional or not, *sub specie aeternitatis.*

It may be instructive to mention a few examples:

Curtailment Suetonius tells of how the Emperor Domitian, angered by certain passages in the History of Hermogenes of Tarsus, not only had the author executed but also crucified the booksellers who distributed the volume. Every Roman library was purified of Hermogenes' book.

Destruction Like so many other invaders, the Turks attempted to destroy the culture of the peoples they conquered. In 1526, the soldiers of the Turkish army set fire to the Great Corvina Library, founded by Matthias Corvinus and said to be one of the jewels of the Hungarian crown. Almost three centuries later, in 1806, their descendants emulated them by burning the extraordinary Fatimid Library in Cairo, containing over 100,000 volumes dating back to the early Middle Ages.

Plunder In 1702, the scholar Arni Magnusson learned that the impoverished inhabitants of Iceland, starving and naked under Danish rule, had raided the ancient libraries of their country, in which unique copies of the *Eddas* had been kept for over 600 years, in order to turn the poetic parchment into winter clothes. Alerted to this act of vandalism, King Frederick IV of Denmark ordered Magnusson to sail to Iceland and rescue the precious manuscripts. Ten years it took Magnusson to strip the thieves and reassemble the collection which, even though soiled and tailored, was shipped back to Copenhagen, where it was carefully guarded

Jaffna library, gutted during an offensive by Sri Lankan government forces –
Credit: Tamil Information Centre

until 1728, when a fire reduced it to illiterate ashes.

Loot Shortly before the end of World War II, in 1945, a Russian officer discovered in an abandoned German railway station a number of open crates overflowing with Russian books and papers which the Nazis had looted. This, according to Ilya Ehrenburg, was all that was left of the celebrated Turgenev Library which the author of *Fathers and Sons* had founded in Paris in 1875, for the benefit of émigré students, and which Nina Berberova called 'the greatest Russian library in exile'.

Banning In March of 1996, the French minister of culture, Philippe Dousre-Blazy, ordered the inspection of the municipal library of Orange, a city ruled since June 1995 by the far-right-wing party of Jean-Marie Le Pen. The report, published three months later, concluded that the Orange librarians were under orders from the mayor to withdraw certain books and magazines from the library shelves: any publications of which Le Pen's party might disapprove, any books by authors critical of the National Front Party, certain foreign literature (North African folk tales, for example) that were considered not part of true French cultural heritage.

Will libraries always exist under such uncertainties? Perhaps not. It may be that virtual libraries may circumvent some of these threats: space would no longer justify culling, since cyberspace is practically infinite, and censorship would no longer affect every one of a library's users, since a censor, circumscribed to one administration and one place, cannot prevent a reader from calling up a forbidden text on a faraway screen in another city, beyond the censor's rule. The electronic media will not, however, be able to circumvent all threats because, in spite of appearances, paper and ink are still more durable than the evanescent letters flickering behind the screen: witness the finite life span of an electronic disk compared with the brittle but death-defying ashes of a papyrus rescued from Pompei and still legible, 19 centuries later, between glass panes at the Archeological Museum in Naples.

I trust that book-burners' dreams are haunted by such modest proofs of the book's survival. ❏

Alberto Manguel is the author of A History of Reading *for which he was awarded the Prix Médici. His latest book is* Into the Looking-Glass Wood (Bloomsbury March 1999)

IVAN KLIMA

A benefactor of the library

He never wished to run anything or do anything other than, at the post office where he worked, sort all the incoming mail correctly. He was conscientious in his work; he even improved the procedure for handling parcels and he never made a mistake. His superiors noticed his conscientiousness and felt that it would be a pity if such a conscientious worker were to spend his whole life sorting mail. They sent him on a course and appointed him librarian in the postal library. There, too, he worked with exemplary conscientiousness. When the director of the district library retired, the postmaster, who sat on the town council, proposed the conscientious man for the new vacancy. There was no other proposal and so the man's appointment went through.

When, on the first day in his new post, the conscientious man entered the library, everything seemed to be in good order. The books on the shelves, in their yellowish-grey covers with clearly legible lettering on their spines: Amado before Amis and Eliot after Eliade. Pinned up on the softboard by the door were seven dust-jackets announcing the latest acquisitions, and a sad-faced woman librarian in a blue overall was entering them in the catalogue.

Leaning against a tidy desk, the new director watched the children and old ladies quietly changing their books. It was all based on some ancient and permanent order that seemed perfect, except that he knew it was not. There was a lot that could be improved in library routine and it certainly was not just a matter of new technology.

That same day, when the last old lady had left with her bundle, he called a meeting of his two subordinates. They were meek ladies who had worked in the library for many years. He tried to discover from them what they thought could be improved in library practice, and he had even equipped himself with a new notepad for their ideas. But the ladies failed to come up with any revolutionary proposals.

He therefore let them go home and himself paced for some time between the stacks, looking at the tidily arranged spines, all the same colour with their legible lettering, and reflected on the changes he would introduce.

Such ordinary books, he reflected, but our entire learning is based on them, for better or worse, and where would all our scholars, artists or even politicians be without them?

He realised that he was now the lord and master of these books, and if one of those celebrities came in he would be able to find them the book they wanted and, in a sense, have a share in their work. But, he reflected with alarm, suppose the book they wanted was unavailable because some unimportant student or old-age pensioner had just borrowed it?

That sort of thing must not be allowed to happen. Surely there were readers who should have precedence over other readers? For instance a teacher over his pupils. And the headmaster over his teachers. And an inspector over headmasters. And the minister over inspectors.

He sat down at a desk, tore a sheet from his notepad and spent a long time drawing up tables.

On the following morning he handed a circular to his two subordinates:

As of today's date, a categorisation of readers into the following categories comes into effect:

Category 1: Pupils at nursery schools

Category 2: Pupils (boys and girls) at general-education schools

Category 3: Pupils (boys and girls) at specialised schools

Category 4: Old-age pensioners and persons of similar standing

Category 5: Citizens only exceptionally working with books, such as barbers, officers, non-commissioned officers and butchers

Category 6: Citizens predominantly working with books, such as teachers, cultural workers, members of amateur circles, as well as doctors and other intellectuals

Category 7: Deserving citizens of local importance, such as heads of schools, pharmacists or the director of our renowned brewery

Category 8: Particularly deserving citizens of local importance, such as the chairmen of political parties, the mayor, the director of the hospital and the players of our famous football club insofar as they may resort to our library

Category 9: Particularly deserving citizens of national importance insofar as they may resort to our library

Category 10: Government ministers, deputy ministers and generals insofar as they may resort to our library.

A member of a lower category may only borrow a book provided no one from a higher category, or even the highest category, has expressed an interest in it. In this way, and in this way alone, can we ensure that a book gets primarily into the most competent hands.

(Signed) The Director of the Library

The two subordinates spent a long time studying the circular. They were accustomed to discipline and order, without which no library can function properly, and therefore did not issue any books that day. Toward evening, one of them ventured to complain to the director: 'In this way we can't issue any books to anyone at all...'

'Why not?' The director expressed surprise. Then he sent them home and for a long time paced between the shelves with their thousands of books all the same colour. Evidently it was not enough to categorise the readers, he reflected; I will have to categorise the books as well. After all, it is highly unlikely that a general would borrow Macha's *May* or Milton's *Paradise Lost*. However, he might, confused by the title, ask for *War and Peace* or Norman Mailer's *The Naked and the Dead,* while this latter book, because of its erotic scenes, should be kept from readers of Categories 1 to 3 altogether. What really mattered was not that everybody should get the book he or she happened to want – that was not even possible – but that they should get the book that was most suitable for them.

The following day he handed his two subordinates his circular No.2:

As of today's date a categorisation of books and pamphlets into the following categories comes into effect

Category A: Books suitable for children and juveniles

Category B: Books suitable for children, juveniles and women

Category C: Books suitable for children, juveniles, women and soldiers

Category D: Books suitable for adults except women and soldiers

Category E: Books suitable for particularly adult readers

Category F: Books suitable for deserving citizens of our town

Category G: Books suitable for particularly deserving citizens of national importance insofar as they may resort to our library

    Category H: Books suitable for government ministers, deputy ministers and generals insofar as they may resort to our library

    Category I: Unsuitable books

    The category of each book shall be clearly marked by a circular rubber stamp.

    (Signed) The Director of the Library

    As soon as they had read the circular the two librarians began to categorise the books. That day, of course, the library remained closed to the general public. Towards evening, the director realised that with his

Credit: Erica Baum/D'Amelio Terras Gallery, New York

present staff the categorisation and marking of the books would take 17 years, and even that only on the assumption that no time would be lost by issuing books or other activities. However, a more serious problem arose. His two subordinates could only assess books for categories A and B, possibly perhaps up to category C; he himself, in all modesty, permitted himself to assess books up to category F. So who would judge the books for the higher categories?

He sent his two subordinates home and for a long time paced between the stacks. The room had already lost some of its former appearance. The books were piled in irregular heaps labelled with capital letters. The world had been created from chaos, and the chaos here merely heralded a new, more perfect order, created for the benefit of all readers.

The director sat down at a desk, tore a sheet from his notepad, trimmed its edges and began a letter to the ministry, justifying his need for more employees.

After a fortnight, three new female librarians and one male librarian turned up at the library. The director issued an important addendum to circular No.2:

Category J: Books suitable for assessors

As well as circular No.3:

As of today's date a double-shift operation will be introduced in order to speed up the overhaul of the activity of our library. Issue of books is hereby suspended until further notice.
The Director of the Library

The library was rapidly losing whatever remained of its old appearance. The room now resembled a large and splendid post office. The books towered to the ceiling in dozens of different coloured pyramids. Between them the assessors walked about in long white overalls, rubber stamps in their hands. The director of the library meanwhile sat alone in his newly equipped office, formerly the children's reading room, with the eleventh pyramid in front of him. This consisted of books on which the assessors could not or dared not agree. After all, assessors were only human.

Humans were fallible. The director realised this and the realisation frightened him. What terrified him most was the thought that even in the 10 piles already assessed and rubber-stamped, mistakes were undoubtedly lurking – mistakes that could nullify the enormous, the infinite, work they had all, jointly, invested.

But the job once started had to be completed. He had no doubt of that. From his desk drawer he took a headed sheet of writing paper and wrote a personal letter to the minister.

Shortly afterwards there arrived another three male librarians and one female one.

To the addendum to circular No 2 the director now issued a further important addendum:

Category K: Books suitable only for super-assessors

When, a short while later, the director of the library died all the books had been categorised into 15 categories. All that remained was for the staff, most ingeniously composed of sub-assessors, assessors, specialised assessors and super-assessors under the leadership of a supreme super-assessor, to carry out a final complete revision.

The director's funeral was attended by several dozen of the library staff. None of the local citizens attended: they had long forgotten that they once had a library in town.

Nonetheless the grateful library staff ordered a a gravestone in the form of an open book to be inscribed:

Here rests a benefactor of the library

Shortly afterwards, books once more began to be lent and borrowed in the town. ❏

Ivan Klíma's *latest novel is* The Ultimate Intimacy *(1998)*

Translated from the Czech by Ewald Osers

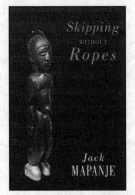

LUCIANO CANFORA

The vanished library

The fate of the Great Library of Alexandria weaves in and out of legend and remains the subject of scholarly wrangles to this day

L arge libraries were first established during the third century BC in the huge area which stretched from Egypt to Syria and Asia Minor. Their reliance on political power is clear from the links between the royal palaces and the libraries, first seen in Alexandria. This 'model' was to remain influential for a long time and peaked during the Arab–Byzantine period, both at Byzantium and Baghdad.

The new concept of the library on a grand scale was an important advance on developments in the Greek city states. It was based on the Aristotelian school, which to a certain extent foreshadowed the royal palace-library model, in its links with the Macedonian monarchy, links which went beyond the merely theoretical. Obviously, the 'Great Library' required financial support and a collections strategy. Before the Ptolemies became the first to do this on a large scale, tracing a 'distant' book was problematic and time-consuming. Proclus relates that when Plato wished to have a text of the poetic works of Antimachus of Colophon, Heraclides had to bring it in person from Asia Minor.[1]

The precedents established by the school of Aristotle and its links with Alexandria are important. It should be remembered that the Ptolemies took power in Egypt as 'foreign' sovereigns in a country that had its own ancient, time-honoured structures. Adjacent to the wall of a tomb in the mausoleum of Rameses II, described by Diodorus Siculus in the first century BC, and just next to the room in which the king was buried, was the 'sacred library', bearing the inscription 'Cure for the Soul'.[2] Nothing similar could be imagined in the humble Greek city

Architect's sketch for the new library at Alexandria
— Credit: Snøhetta

states. At best, private libraries were set up on a small scale, such as the one Euripides is said to have owned. This was so in Athens, but Athens was exceptional.

The Aristotelian model was clearly in evidence in the Great Royal Library of Alexandria. The Museum there was particularly important, with a community of scholars rigorously recruited by the king. In the Museum precinct, there were shelves for the scrolls; this formed the Great Library, which had its own organisational structure and served, firstly, the scholars of the Museum. As with the Aristotelian school, the Museum was a *thiasos* of scholars united by the cult of the Muses. Strabo describes the Museum in his *Geography*, informing us that the scholars held common ownership of their possessions and that one was appointed a 'priest of the Museum' by the ruler (the emperor Augustus in Strabo's time).[3]

The fact that the Museum was considered one of the 'wonders' of Alexandria is clear from the *First Mimiambos* of Herondas (vv 26–32). Herondas was almost certainly active under Philadelphus (285–246), therefore during the library's greatest splendour. He returns to the Museum in the *Eighth Mimiambos*, where he writes about his *Dream* and foresees that the scholars 'caught up with the Muses' would undo all his work. The Sceptic Timon of Phlius, who also flourished during the time of Philadelphus, however, speaks with derision of the scholars supported by the king of Egypt in the Museum: 'In the populous land of Egypt,' he says in one of his *silli* (short satirical pieces in hexameters), 'literary runts are kept who squabble eternally in the cage of the Muses.'

The Museum had its 'keeper' (*epistates*) who, in the same way as the Peripatetic scholastics, oversaw research which was expanding in various areas. When, under Philadelphus, the library took on huge dimensions and needed its own director, one of the Museum scholars, appointed by the palace, took on the function of *prostates* (leader) of the library. It was an official post, often mentioned in the Byzantine lexicon *Suidas* in the biographies of the scholars who succeeded to the post (Callimachus, Zenodotus, Apollonius Rhodius, Eratosthenes etc).

Despite the prestige of the Library of Alexandria, very few sources of the Hellenistic period explicitly mention it. The first reference comes in the *Letter of Aristeas* (which probably dates to around the middle of the second century BC); this reference is an isolated one; alongside it are found the papyrus which provides a list of librarians[4] and, from the

Byzantine period, Tzetzes' references to comedy in his *Prolegomena*.

The increasing numbers of literary texts, systematically acquired on the wishes of Ptolemy Philadelphus, called for expert textual scholars (known as *philologoi*), who had to deal with complicated problems of cataloguing and of attribution. The best known and most impressive cataloguing procedure (promoted by Callimachus) was drawing up the *Pinakes* (catalogues of proven authors from various disciplines with a list of their works). From the few remaining fragments, we can gain an idea of the problems, particularly those of authenticating the collections that found their way to the library, and with which Callimachus and his collaborators had to deal. Amongst the information appearing in these catalogues was the calculation of the number of lines (known as stichometry): this was used to protect the original text and to reveal any changes. The Alexandrians did not invent this system but they brought it into general use. From a passage in Theopompus, we learn that he himself provided, in a preface, the stichometry of his work as an orator (20,000 lines) and as a historian (150,000 lines).[5] Evidence of stichometry is also found in Byzantine manuscripts of the ninth to the eleventh centuries.

One of the practical aspects of the expansion of the library was the adoption of larger scrolls. This can be seen in the remains of a work which was produced at Alexandria alongside the growing library: the *Elements* by Euclid. Here volume X, far more extensive than the previous volumes, is not limited to presenting, as in the other volumes, the *Definitions*, but also presents, in the main body of the book, his second and third books of *Definitions* (vol. III, pp.136 and 256 Heiberg's edition). This book is clearly composed of three scrolls, which together form a scroll of larger proportions.[6] The fact that Euclid worked and taught in Alexandria shows that it was there that this innovation must have been seen first. The expansion of the size of books sheds some light on the polemical formulation of Callimachus regarding the 'great books' (defined by him as the 'great scourge'). Books were now commonly much larger than those in the previous period, a change which also influenced writing practices. Consider, for example, that the epic poem of Apollonius Rhodius (the *Argonautica*) – to which the Callimachus dispute referred – is almost three times as long as a typical Homeric text.

Around the same time as Callimachus, libraries were established in two other cities, Antioch and Pergamum, under the Seleucids and the

Attalids respectively. A sign of the rivalry between Alexandria and Pergamum is the information, derived from the great scholar Varro, perhaps from his lost *De Bibliothecis*, that Ptolemy allegedly had recourse to an embargo on the export of papyrus. But the rivalry was particularly evident in the way in the way in which the scholars of the two great centres believed classical texts should be studied.

According to tradition – a tradition widely held – the largest and best library in the Greco-Roman world, the Library of Alexandria, was set on fire during Caesar's dramatic campaign against Ptolemy XIII, known as the 'Alexandrian War' (48–47BC). However, neither *Bellum Alexandrinum* nor Cicero, among other contemporary sources, say anything about this (hypothetical) event. A historian of the next generation, Titus Livius (Livy), who was only 18-years-old at the time of the alleged fire, spoke of the loss of 40,000 scrolls.[7] If these were indeed scrolls from the Library, this would have been a tenth of the total number, which amounted to 500,000 or even 700,000 scrolls. Plutarch, who wrote about 150 years after these events, certainly believed this to be so and said that the fire at the port 'caused damage to the Great Library'.[8] We do not know if they really were scrolls from the Library. One might wonder why they were at the dockyard, next to stores of grain.[9] It has not been ruled out that these were actually scrolls for export.

We know what Livy said from Seneca, who quotes him and paraphrases him. According to Seneca – he read Livy in full – the books were 'a beautiful symbol of the opulence' of the kings of Egypt. He does not say that they formed a part of the Great Library. His nephew Lucan, in his epic historic poem on the civil war between Caesar and Pompey (also based on Livy), while quite hostile to Caesar and very detailed in its description of the fire at the port of Alexandria, does not mention the burning of books. This omission is significant. If, however, precious and valuable books were burned because they were stored at the port near to the stores of grain, one would rightly ask oneself why they were there. According to certain sources, Caesar, in the first part of his stay in Alexandria, made lengthy visits to philosophers and scholars who, perhaps, frequented the Museum or were guardians of the library.[10] It is likely that he then thought of founding a large public library to be entrusted to Varro, and that he requested the kings who were his hosts to send several thousands of scrolls (or to have copies made) from the library to Rome.[11] This may be why the scrolls were in storage at the port at the time of the fire, waiting to be sent off.

Centuries later, sources which dazzle with their own confusion, speak of the destruction of the 'entire patrimony' of the library.[12] But, they are not now considered reliable. Neither does the 'rumour' – as Plutarch defines it[13] – according to which Mark Antony (before 31BC) was said to have given Cleopatra 200,000 scrolls from the library of Pergamum, provide any evidence of the assumed destruction of the Library of Alexandria. If this were true, it could be seen as exaggerated compensation for damage which was not serious.

In any case, about 20 years after the Alexandrian War, Strabo visited Alexandria and gives a magnificent description of the Museum.[14] From what he writes one can deduce that, at that time (25BC), there was still a properly functioning library. The way he writes implies that everything was in the right place: the Museum, the *peripatum* (along which were the shelves), the residences of the scholars and the communal dining hall. During the reign of Claudius (41–54AD), on the

initiative of the scholar-emperor who was also respected as a historian, a
new museum was constructed at Alexandria: it was placed alongside 'the
old Museum' – according to Suetonius – and was called Claudianum.[15]
It is now clear that, in referring to 'the old Museum', Suetonius means
the one from the Ptolemaic period, which still existed during Claudius's
time.

A few years later, Domitian (81-96AD) sent to Alexandria a team of
copyists and philologists to copy the books in the library with the aim of
replenishing other libraries (presumably those in Rome), that had been
damaged by fire.[16] In the reign of Marcus Aurelius, an Egyptian
document, dated 31 March 173AD, speaks of a certain Valerius
Diodorus, 'deputy librarian and member of the Museum'.[17] His name
appears in another document, also of Egyptian origin.[18] Here a rich
gentleman, also a scholar, speaks of books which he wanted to have
copied, and he says that those books were to be found at the office of
'Diodorus and his group'. These documents refer to the library and to
the Museum, mentioning the name of one of those in charge of the
'library service'.

Several years later, the great scholar Athenaeus was active in Egypt at
Naucrates. He wrote a book, *The Scholars at Table*, which gives the
impression that there was such a wealth of old books, Attic comedies and
histories, that one supposes that this fortunate scholar had access to
important collections of 'classics', already about six centuries old. Which
would they be if not the ones from the Museum?

We know certainly when the end of those old collections came:
around 70 years after Athenaeus, when Alexandria was the scene of a
ferocious war between the emperor Aurelian (270-275 AD) and Queen
Zenobia. 'In the reign of Aurelian,' wrote Ammianus Marcellinus,
during the course of the civil war, most of the district known as
'Bruchion' was destroyed.[19] It was the quarter where the old palace was
located, inside of which was the Great Library.

That something survived those ruins is proved by the fact that, in the
time of Theodosius (who died in 395AD), an Egyptian scholar known as
Theon was described as 'the man from the Museum'.[20] It was this
'modern' reincarnation of the library the Arabs found when they
conquered the city of Alexander the Great on 29 September 642 and
became its heirs. ❏

Footnotes:

1 Proclus, *Commentary on the Timaeus, 21c*
2 Diodorus, *Bibliotheca Historica* I. 49, 3–4
3 Strabo, *Geography*, p.794
4 Oxyrhyncus Papyrus 1241. A second library was established in the Serapeum and, therefore, when Epiphanius, an ecclesiastical writer of the fourth century AD mentions the translation of the Septuagint, he states that the work was deposited 'in the first library'
5 Fr. 25 Jacoby
6 Discovered by B. Hemmerdinger
7 Fr. 52 (Weissenborn) = Seneca *Tr. an. 9.5*
8 *Caesar*, 49, 6. More recent writers translate this as 'destroyed' because influenced by later beliefs that the event was catastrophic
9 According to Dio Cassius (42, 38, 2)
10 Appianus, *Civ.* II, 89, 376; cfr Lucan X, 14–20
11 Suetonius, *Caesar* 44
12 These include Ammianus Marcellinus (22,16, 3) and the interpolator who included Aulus Gellius (*Noctes Atticae* VII, 17) with information on the library of Alexandra
13 Plutarch, *Antonius*, 58, 9
14 *Geography* XVII, pp 793–794
15 Suetonius, *Claudius*, 42, 5
16 Suetonius, *Domitian*, 20
17 Merton Papyrus 19 (published by Harold Idris Bell in 1948)
18 Oxyrhyncus Papyrus, 2192
19 Ammianus Marcellinus, *Res Gestae* XXII, 16, 15
20 *Suidas*, entry on *Theon*

Luciano Canfora is professor of classical philology at Bari University, director of the historical journal Quaderni di Storia *and a member of the editorial board of Boston University's* International Journal of the Classical Tradition. *Among his many books,* La biblioteca scomparsa *(1989) has been translated into English as* The Vanished Library *(California University Press). He is currently writing* The Life of Julius Caesar: the Democratic Dictatorship.

Translated by Antonia Coleman

ANDREW HAMMOND

Echoes of lost grandeur

Bibliophiles fear that Egypt's latest 'Grand Project' is in danger of ending up as a collection of symbols rather than of books

After two decades of delay, the countdown has begun to the opening of the new Alexandria Library, or the Bibliotheca Alexandrina (BA), as it is known. Egypt expects a media event of mega-proportions, probably in October and almost certainly by the end of the year: President Hosni Mubarak is due for 're-election' to a fourth term in October, and Federico Mayor, president of UNESCO and a major backer of the scheme, ends his term at the end of the year.

But many involved in the project believe that, unless there is a huge injection of cash, the library has little chance of being more than a monument to a once great city with a once great library. It has cost US$190 million to build and equip and a further US$182 million in government funding for the land, the consultancies and an annual budget for the General Organisation of the Alexandria Library (GOAL). But the dream of a library to rank among the most prestigious in history is unlikely to be realised.

Dr Mohsen Zahran, GOAL's head, says that 320,000 titles have been obtained in book and electronic form. The official publicity talked of a target of 8 million in a decade's time. Zahran seems to acknowledge that it may not happen. 'It won't just be a library,' he says, 'since it will include extra features such as an audio-visual section, a business centre and a display of archaeological finds from the site the library stands on. And in any case, it's not size, it's the quality that matters.'

Size may not be everything, but insiders say the acquisitions policy was decided far too late and is way off the mark. GOAL is proud that individuals and organisations have donated material from all over the world and there is much of note. Spain donated the Escorial collection of Arab writers from Andalusia on microfilm, and manuscripts dating back to the eighth century have been transferred from Alexandria's municipal library. It will also house records of the British presence in Egypt, the Suez Canal and the Ottoman era.

The reliance on random donations, however, has meant that the acquisitions policy has resembled 'Granny's attic being cleared out', as one member of the Friends of the BA puts it. Insiders speak of important elements from the history of Alexandria being omitted, such as the role of its Jewish community. GOAL is also secretive as to precisely what it has acquired. The annual budget for books is only US$30,000 and GOAL insists on buying two of every title. 'The BA should establish an endowment for book-buying,' says Professor Mohammed M Aman, a consultant from the University of Wisconsin-Milwaukee.

Whatever its shortcomings, the BA will stand out a mile in a country where the state of public and academic libraries is generally appalling. The *Dar Al Kutub* in Cairo, which houses 5 million volumes, is crying out for a major overhaul. The BA also aims to be all things to all men: a public library for Alexandrians, a resource for Alexandria University and a research centre for scholars world-wide.

Egypt has always had a partiality for the 'Grand Project', and this one is supported by the president's wife, Suzanne Mubarak, patron of the national literacy campaign, 'Reading for All'. Critics say that two other libraries she has been associated with are more sensible examples of how to spend money. The non-lending Greater Cairo Library was built in an old royal palace for E£7 million (just over US$2 million) and holds 150,000 volumes, mainly on modern Egyptian history but with special collections on Cairo. The Mubarak Public Library holds 95,000 volumes and is the largest children's library in the country. 'They are small, strategically-located and quite impressive,' says John Rodenbeck, professor of ancient Mediterranean history at the American University in Cairo (AUC). 'But I don't see the benefit of the Alexandria Library for Alexandria.'

In the last generation, Alexandria has become a battered and overcrowded city of around six million, where services have deteriorated to crisis levels. A new governor was appointed last year with a reformist mandate and the library opening will coincide with a looked-for revival.

Despite fears about holes in the growing collection, it is hoped the BA will be a bulwark in a cultural climate that is tetchy on freedom of expression. This year the religious establishment, in the form of Al Azhar University, caused the celebrated novel *A Place Under the Sun* by Egyptian writer Ahdaf Soueif, Mohamed Choukri's *For Bread Alone* and a biography of Prophet Mohammed by Marxist historian Maxime Rodinson to be removed from the library of the AUC [see In the News p12].

Perhaps it was churlish of the man who first floated the idea of reviving the ancient library of Alexandria in the 1970s to have turned against it 20 years later. The point at which Dr Mustafa Al Abbadi, a Greco-Roman historian at Alexandria University, got off was at the clearing of the site, in the old Royal Quarter district where the original library is thought to have stood. After the Norwegian architectural firm Snøhetta won the design competition, work began in 1992, without first excavating the site for antiquities. The site was 'massacred', in the words of prominent Alexandrian architect Mohammed Awad.

The design is wonderfully ripe with symbolism. A vast disc arises from a pit by the sea front, with 40 metres of structure above ground and 40 below. The outer walls will be decorated with scrambled letters from hundreds of alphabets. The symbolism of digging into the earth and gradually uncovering the gradations of history, is reflected in the layers of terraces housing the collections. ❑

Andrew Hammond is a freelance writer based in Cairo, and deputy editor of the bi-weekly Cairo Times *magazine. He writes on political and cultural issues in Egypt and the Middle East*

Construction underway at the new Alexandria library
– Credit: Trygve Bølstad/Panos

Index and the Norwegian Forum for Freedom of Expression have compiled a database on freedom of expression in the twentieth century, to be handed over to the Alexandria Library when it opens in autumn 1999 ❏

word power

from *Auto-Da-Fé*, Elias Canetti
translated by CV Wedgwood

Eratosthenes, the great librarian of Alexandria, a scholar of universal significance who flourished in the third century of the pre-Christian era and held sway over more than half a million manuscript scrolls, made in his eightieth year a terrible discovery. His eyes began to refuse their office. He could still see but he could not read. Another man might have waited until he was completely blind. He felt that to take leave of his books was blindness enough. Friends and pupils implored him to stay with them. He smiled wisely, thanked them, and in a few days starved himself to death.

Should the time come this great example could easily be followed even by the lesser Kien, whose library comprised a mere twenty-five thousand volumes...

His library was situated on the fourth and topmost floor of No.24 Ehrlich Strasse. The door of the flat was secured by three highly complicated locks. He unlocked them, strode across the hall, which contained nothing except an umbrella and coat-stand, and entered his study. Carefully he set down the brief-case on an armchair. Then once and again he paced the entire length of the four lofty, spacious communicating rooms which formed his library. The entire wall-space up to the ceiling was clothed with books. Slowly he lifted his eyes towards them. Skylights had been let into the ceiling. He was proud of his roof-lighting. The windows had been walled up several years before after a determined struggle with his landlord. In this way he had gained in every room a fourth wall-space: accommodation for more books. Moreover illumination from above, which lit up all the shelves equally, seemed to him more just and suited to his relations with his books. The temptation to watch what went on in the street – an immoral and time-wasting habit – disappeared with the side windows. Daily, before he sat down to his writing desk, he blessed both the idea and its results, since he owed to them the fulfilment of his dearest wish: the possession of a well-stocked library, in perfect order and enclosed on all sides, in which no single superfluous article of furniture, no single superfluous person could lure him from his serious thoughts. ❏

SONALLAH IBRAHIM

There's no beating that devil

For a prisoner, every victory is a great victory, and where books are prohibited, every book is a great book

Mention Cairo and an image of the citadel springs to mind, the picture reproduced in guidebooks and on stamps: two graceful minarets hugging a dome. They are part of the mosque that Muhammad Ali built onto Salah ed-Din's original fortress in the middle of the last century. As all his predecessors had done, this reckless Albanian added structures to the citadel that he thought would keep him in the minds of his people and preserve his memory for posterity.

The British, too, apparently respected this tradition when they occupied Egypt in 1882, contributing their own view of how they wanted to be remembered. Inside, they constructed a small jail for political prisoners, the last inmates of which were the Islamic extremists who killed Anwar al-Sadat in 1981. Perhaps the Egyptian government felt guilty about their role in executing these killers, for not long afterwards, they closed down the prison and turned it into a police museum.

The prison–museum consists of a long block above which, built along the sides of two open passageways, a line of small cells is attached. In four of these cells, life-sized figures dressed in appropriate clothes represent Mamelouk, Ottoman, Mohammed Alid and modern prisoners. In the first three cells, the models are shackled to stakes with iron chains. The picture changes dramatically in the fourth, where we find the model in contemporary clothing (shirt and trousers), wearing glasses and holding a book. This picture betrays its creator's grasp of the connection between revolt and awareness. Sadly, the picture lacks historical accuracy.

I know this from personal experience that dates from the beginning of
1959.

It was seven years after the Egyptian revolution, which had swept
away every facet of the *anciene régime* by abolishing the monarchy and
expelling the British from the land. Despite the confrontation over Suez,
Gamal Abdel Nasser did not lose faith in the possibility of cooperation
with the West. Representatives of the youthful Egyptian administration
went to the USA and West Germany, but the security delegation
returned to Egypt with little more than advanced ideas about how to
deal with the political prisoner. Top of the list of innovations was to
deny him so much as a piece of paper, a pen or a book. And how
successfully the Egyptian administration applied this western knowledge
when Nasser staged his notorious campaign against the Left.

This was how I found myself one night entering the cavernous
citadel by one of its ancient wooden doors and coming to rest in the
small English jail, in none other than the above-mentioned cell. The
guards left me my clothes and my glasses, but they were intent on
keeping from me anything that I might use to read or write.

After three months, our number had swollen and the cells of the
small prison shrunk, so they transferred us to the main district prison.
Overcrowding brought us into close contact with the ordinary prisoners,
and this brought us, in turn, the opportunity to obtain newspapers and
books. In fact, the prison had a vast library of all kinds of books in
different languages, created over decades by contributions from the
inmates themselves, who had comprised a fair proportion of educated
people and foreigners. We threatened to go on hunger strike if not
allowed to use the library, and the administration agreed to allow one of
us to borrow a handful of books and distribute them among our cells.

Of course it was impossible to control the choice our representative
made, even as he tried to satisfy our various tastes. This was how I got
the chance to read books I could never have chosen for myself, so far
were they from my sphere of interest. I was 21 and still obsessed by
thrillers, not political books, which I read with little enthusiasm. I read
about al-Muttanabbi and al-Maari in Taha Hussein, and erotic stories by
Mazeni that were not in general circulation. I still remember the simply
designed yellow cover of Robert Graves's *I Claudius*, with its publisher's
mark of an albatross. I also read in English a unique work by a writer
with a Dutch name that I can no longer recall, its subject the same

60 INDEX ON CENSORSHIP 2 1999

geography that had concealed such horrors for me at school; the writer engaged me with his elegance of style and lightness of touch, and made me realise that even the most difficult and complex subjects could be transformed into a delightful story if the writer was cultivated, passionate about his subject and intent on conveying it to others. I also became acquainted with architecture and the accomplishments of Frank Lloyd Wright, through the story 'The Fountainhead', by the American conservationist Ayn Rand. And it may have been the writing of Axel Munthe that sowed in my mind the seed for the series of stories I wrote 20 years later about the animal world.

These books lightened our troubles. We lived in small cells, each with room only for three metal bunk beds. Insects prevented us from sleeping, so we spent the night reading and slept during the day. But the experts did not rest until they had moved us to a segregated prison and forbidden books altogether.

Once more we resorted to blackmail by going on hunger strike. But this time the authorities ignored the strikers until, after 24 days, they were close to death and had to stop. So we tried another ruse, unashamedly exploiting a traditional respect for religion. We had Muslims, Christians and Jews among us, and it was not in the power of the prison governor to refuse their requests for their Holy Books. So I read the Quran, the Torah and the Gospels from cover to cover. I believe this was one of the most formative things I ever did, for it showed me the inviolable relationship between the three books and their different divine revelations of the ancient human dream for justice and equality. With the tales of the Torah and the Quran I also felt in myself a thirst for stories; my imagination leapt upon them with great energy. I believe it was then that I began to think of writing as a vocation.

After a period of moving from one prison to another, interspersed with bouts of physical torture, we arrived in a military detention centre deep in the desert, about 400 kilometres from the banks of the Nile. Here were hundreds of detainees, in total isolation.

Satiated by Holy Books, we resorted to 'audio-books'. For it emerged that some of our group had powerful memories of what they had read, and these stories they told. Some became stars in the cells. They were smuggled from one cell to another for one more night of entertainment.

But such banishment creates an environment of its own that no outside authority will master. The guards, soldiers and officers here were also imprisoned, by the formidable distance that separated them from civilisation. Inevitably, with time, human relationships grew between us. We convinced them to bring a few books when they came back from their holidays and to bury them outside in the desert. Later, they would bring them into the prison, to be kept in hiding places underground.

Once again, we had little control over what was brought us, for you cannot give a semi-illiterate guard a list of required titles. Instead, we'd give him the address of a relation, and a message asking for any books they might have to spare. Once again I found myself with a superabundance of books of extraordinarily different kinds, from a story about the Nazi concentration camps by Apitz, to an exposition of relativity theory. I remember being like a radar that moved in every direction to pick up whatever might stimulate my imagination.

However, the arrival of some books was particularly thrilling, like the day when the Naguib Mahfouz trilogy appeared straight from the press. Our colleague in charge of distribution had a list of requests recorded with a burnt stick on the bottom of a cigarette packet. When I hastened to put down my name for the trilogy, I found a long queue of people had reserved it before me. Sick people had priority for the few luxuries of our shared life, so I made out that I was ill. But then I discovered a large number of sick people on the list in front of me who needed the diversion only the Mahfouz trilogy could afford. I devised a new pretext, and made out that I was committed to writing a series of literary papers and needed to read the trilogy as a matter of urgency. Imagine my astonishment when I found a not inconsiderable number of colleagues had declared that they, too, were giving papers on literary writing and all needed to sharpen their faculties by reading this same novel.

I was not exactly lying when I used my literary projects as an excuse. I had begun to think of myself as a writer and did write scores of stories and novels - in my head! It was not long before I felt restricted by this and began to look out for any means of acquiring paper and pen. The plan to wear us down included a policy of forced labour, breaking stones. As there was only sand in the area, and nothing for us to do, we persuaded the administration to 'force us' to grow plants and supply the prison with the vegetables it needed. One morning, lorries dumped masses of cement in the area where we were to build cisterns for irrigation. By evening, the cement sacks were up in the cells, where they were torn into sheets of writing paper. It wasn't difficult to get hold of small pieces of lead pencil. Suddenly I was able to write my first story.

Writing took place in the evening, after lockup, when the guards retreated to their nearby quarters. The hiding places would open and each would take up his book or his 'sack' with its distinctive damp smell. About halfway through the night it would all go back into hiding. Despite an awareness of the importance of creative writing, it was only natural that what I did should be thought less significant than the writing of Party and political papers. Occasionally, whoever was in charge would declare that there wasn't room in the hiding places for my handful of stories, and that it would have to be destroyed. To guarantee a place for my work I took responsibility for the things hidden in my cell. One night, as I was getting the papers out, the guards staged a surprise search and caught me red-handed.

The guard took me to the director's office. In my wake came a few of the prison characters who normally represented us when we dealt with the administration. The ensuing confrontation reflected the new balance of power in the prison. Our representatives defended our right to possess books and threatened revolt if a finger was laid upon us or our books confiscated. The director decided to withdraw quietly and disregard what had happened, and I returned victorious with my books and papers.

Our situation had also improved thanks to an easing of the country's political situation and the widening influence of the international protest movement against our imprisonment. Better-quality paper appeared in the shape of school exercise books, there were enough pens to go round even for the young writers. It became possible to transcribe work, in minute writing, onto cigarette papers, and to smuggle it out. I began to think about a full-length novel and kept a notebook in which I recorded my thoughts, plans for stories and notes on books I was reading and those I wanted to read. By good fortune I was able to smuggle out the better part of this notebook.

One section, beginning in June 1964, contains extracts of a letter from Hemingway to Scott Fitzgerald saying that anything afflicting the writer must be of potential use and, if it causes pain, he must not complain but turn the pain into work. I also recorded his advice to the writer always to record what he sees or hears. Another entry comments on a novel by Virginia Woolf: 'To the Lighthouse has opened up a new world to me. I read without ever knowing exactly what the story is, and all the while feelings and extraordinary sensations open up inside me.' There were extracts from Proust, Hegel, the aging Stravinsky on reaching 90, *La Peste*, *Of Human Bondage* and many others.

The most obvious result that this reading bred in me was my desire to have my own book. There was by now an extensive publishing operation in the prison. Priority went to political books and to those in which the most prominent figures participated. The calligrapher, who wrote the text and titles in a beautiful hand, accepted payment in the form of a certain number of cigarettes. If the author was lucky, illustrations would be done by one of the interned artists, among whom was the late Hassan Fu'ad, who'd played such a major role in the development of book cover design before his arrest. After that, the books were bound with dismantled cardboard boxes and glued with paste made from bread flour.

Such lengths were not gone to for anyone, particularly not a young, novice writer like me. So I gave up part of my daily share of cigarettes and bought paper and the transcribing and binding services. One copy of a small booklet of four short stories was the result. Then our colleagues decided to stage an exhibition of the books that had been produced inside the prison. Hassan Fu'ad presided over their production, with elegant coloured covers some of which he did himself. Abdel Azeem Anise graciously invited me to share his notebook for the exhibition.

The exhibition happened during one of the feasts, when there was less supervision and the prison governor was away. The books were arranged on boxes covered in cloth and put on show in the corridor between the cells. There were two novels by Ibrahim Abdel Halim and a play by Salah Hafez with an introduction by Hassan Fu'ad, a translation of a Soviet science fiction novel and a study of the 1919 revolution. There were also collections of stories and poems, and a number of new political translations. And in the middle of this collection with its stylish covers sat my second book. My chance to be properly published had been realised at last.

The publishing continued and flourished until we were transferred to other prisons and eventually released in 1964. But most of what we produced appeared again, in the normal way, in thousands of copies. Our experience left us with the certainty that books always triumph over attempts to ban them or burn and destroy them, because they are a devil you can't beat. ❏

Sonallah Ibrahim *is one of Egypt's most celebrated writers of fiction. One of his novels,* The Smell of It, *informed by his experience of returning to 'normal life' after imprisonment, was censored on publication in 1966 and not published in Arabic in its complete form until 20 years later*

Translated from the Arabic by Rebecca Porteous

MARTIN ESPADA

Prisoner AM-8335 and his Library of Lions

For Mumia Abu-Jamal, SCI-Greene, Waynesburg, PA

When the guards handcuffed inmates in the shower
and shoved them skidding naked to concrete,
or the blue shirts billyclubbed a prisoner
to wrench the gold from his jaw,
to swirl KKK in his spat blood,
the numbered men pressed their fingertips
against the smooth cool pages of your voice,
that voice of many books,
and together you whispered in the yard
about lawsuits, about the newspapers.

From the battlements
the warden trumpeted a proclamation:
in every cell one box per inmate,
twelve by twelve by fourteen,
for all personal possessions. You say
four blue shirts crowded your death row cell
to wrestle seventeen cartons away,
wrinkled paperbacks in pillars
toppling, history or law collected and studied
like the bones of a fossilised predator,
a library beyond Carnegie's whitest visions of marble.

One guard would fondle a book
emblazoned with the word *Revolutionary*, muttering:
This is what we're supposed to get.

Today, after the hunger strike,
you sit windowed in the visiting room,
prisoner AM–8335: dreadlocks blooming
like an undiscovered plant of the rain forest,
hands coupled in the steel cuffs,
brown skin against the striped prison jump-suit,
tapestry of the chain gang.

I would rather be beaten, you say,
than this assault on the life of the mind.
You keep Toni Morrison's book in your box with the toothpaste.
You gaze through the glass at the towering apparition
of your library, as if climbing marble steps.

As you say:
Giving up a book is like giving up a child,
like parting with your own flesh.
How do you choose between *Beloved* and *The Wretched of the Earth*?

Your eyes pool.
A single tear is the scarification of your cheekbone,
a warrior's ceremonial gash on death row.
Across the glass a reflection of the guards walking,
small blue men patrolling your forehead.

In the parking lot, I turn again towards the prison,
walls ribboned with jagged silver loops of wire,
and see a great library
with statues of lions at the gate. ❑

Martín Espada is the author of five poetry collections, including Imagine the
Angels of Bread *(WW Norton), which won the Before Columbus Foundation's*
American Book Award.

AHDAF SOUEIF

Cry havoc

The destruction of a library leaves us all the poorer. Creating one is a way of offering the past a refuge from the present

8 August 1998: My brother is conducting in Sarajevo – in the ruins of the National Library. I have seen photographs of it.

A line from one of the last scenes of a novel I have been working on for two years. One of the most sympathetic characters in the book is Omaral-Ghamrawi, the narrator's brother. A pianist and conductor, he plays for free where disasters have taken place: in Qana, in Beirut, in Sarejevo. I write these lines and then I am on my knees among cardboard boxes of newspaper cuttings, trying to find an article that captured my imagination 18 months ago. In the colour supplement of the *Guardian* there was a double-page photograph of the library in Sarajevo and below it a close-up of a man's face. The man wore dark-rimmed spectacles and his broad smile revealed a crooked central tooth. He was Nikolai Koljevic,the Shakespearean scholar who – the article said – had signed the order on the 25 August 1992 for General Mladic to bomb the library, and who had killed himself on 17 January 1997. A question that has always – perhaps naively – troubled me: if it is true that exposure to art makes better human beings of us, then how can someone who has made the study of literature his life's work do something really terrible? Pinned up on my wall, the burned-out shell of the National Library glooms down on the final pages of my book.

Every morning the newspapers carry images of cruelty and disaster to our doorsteps. What was it about this particular image that had touched me so closely? I study the page, the arched colonnades like an inverted tower of Pisa. To the right of the photo, placed against the far wall, at an angle, turned away slightly from the eye of the viewer, an obscure cuboid structure draws my eye again and again.

Interior of the National Library in Sarajevo. Two million books were destroyed –
Credit: Paul Lowe/Magnum

Growing up in Egypt, one of my earliest – and recurring – history lessons was about the Great Library at Alexandria, a repository of thousands of manuscripts, of all the knowledge of the ancient world, where men like Euclid and Pythagoras studied and formulated their ideas. Burned to the ground – whether by design or accident, the stories differ. But burned it was and we Egyptians learned early to mourn that loss. And growing up in Egypt, I learned also to love libraries and bookshops and feel at home in them. When my father was eighteen he spent a year in one of King Farouq's jails for his leftist leanings. He whiled away the time by translating Aristotle's *Poetics*. Later, in his search for old texts he would take me with him to *Dar al-Kutub*, the Egyptian National Library, or to the musty upper gallery of *al-Nahda* bookshop where Fawzi, the manager, would always order a cold drink for the child who sat quietly with a picture-book while her father rummaged and read. And there was the Anglo-Egyptian Bookshop and Publishing House, where old Sobhi Grace would complain how broke he was and weep with tears as he handed my mother her royalties on some publication of hers but always throw in a gift of a book for me waiting at her side. And then there were the delights of *Surel-Azbakiyyah*: the railings around the old Azbakiyyah gardens where the secondhand book sellers had their stalls. A visit to my grandparents in Ataba always meant a lingering stop and a purchase. There I bought *Little Women*, Charles Lamb's *Tales from Shakespeare*, *What Katy Did*, *Black Beauty* and various collections of nursery rhymes and bedtime stories. I have never been able to pass a row of books without looking through them and I have never been able to throw away even the most tattered of paperbacks.

Today, in my office, images from another Sarajevo library are spread across the desk. The Ghazi-Husrev Beg Library was also bombed. But the staff there managed to rescue the 10,000 manuscripts in their charge. They carried them off in bundles and hid them in cupboards and under beds. Time and again they moved them and when things calmed down in the city they were given an old school for their headquarters and they put the manuscripts down on the floor and looked to the world for help.

The foundation where I have worked for the last 10 years was set up by Sheikh Ahmed Zaki Yamani in 1989 to deal with this kind of problem. The world knows Sheikh Yamani as Saudi Minister of Oil and Chairman of OPEC when OPEC was at the height of its powers. It knows him for being kidnapped by Carlos the Jackal and held hostage for four days. What it perhaps does not know is that he was born in Makkah to a father who had a library of rare manuscripts and who was himself a writer; that he grew up with a love of books and a deep feeling for their value. In 1986, free of public office for the first time in his adult life, the Sheikh set about realising an old dream. From the Yamani Cultural Foundation was born the al-Furqan Islamic Heritage Foundation, a non-profit-making organisation with a brief to work for the preservation of the 3 million or so manuscripts believed to have been written under the aegis of Muslim culture from the ninth to the nineteenth centuries.

The first project al-Furqan undertook was a vast survey of collections of Islamic manuscripts all over the world. This survey was published in four volumes covering 118 countries and was the first such work to list private as well as public collections. Since then, the foundation has set up and administered cataloguing projects in Africa, Asia and eastern Europe. It has published these catalogues and, as a result, several previously unheard of works have been brought into the public realm of scholarship.

Although that *Guardian* photo continues to haunt me, my job with the foundation has taken some of the edge off my feelings of helplessness. At least we are doing something, I can tell myself. When the Ghazi Husrev Beg Library appealed to us for help, we sent them shelving and equipment. We also funded a project to image all their collection onto both micro-film and CD-ROM. Their staff are working three 8-hour shifts a day to complete the project, and the films and CDs have begun to arrive at the foundation headquarters in Wimbledon where they are available to any scholar who wants to study them. Al-Furqan has also set up a preservation council and is about to launch a preservation newsletter. This will provide a network of information for all librarians working with collections of Islamic manuscripts. In addition, the Foundation has run postgraduate courses for cataloguers in Cairo, Istanbul and London and made it possible for librarians from 26 countries to attend them.

Sometimes the task seems endless, but it isn't. Sheikh Yamani's vision is far-reaching, to be sure, but it is a realisable vision: the day will come, we are convinced, when all this important manuscript material is housed in safety. At the very least, al-Furqan offers the past a refuge from the present – and the future.

And so I am immersed in books, working to preserve them in the day, writing them in the night. And one evening, sitting on the floor among the shelves of London's School of Oriental and African Studies library, looking up a last-minute quote from Cromer's *Modern Egypt*, it comes to me: it must have been the school holidays, 40 years ago, when my mother, heavily pregnant with my sister, and trying to make ground with her PhD thesis before the delivery, smuggled me into the North Library in the Senate House. In the SOAS library I see, once again, my six-year-old self, sitting 'quiet as a mouse' by my mother's feet in their sensible, low-heeled shoes, leafing through an illustrated Victorian *Lalla Rookh* in a study cubicle set against the wall at an angle away from the main hall of the library.

At home, I look at the photograph with new recognition as I understand my feelings for that room-like structure which, smoke-marked and doorless retains its angle, its wish for privacy. And I place my character, Omaral-Ghamrawi in the middle of the scene:

8 August 1998:

My brother is conducting in Sarajevo – in the ruins of the National Library. I have seen photographs of it: the high ceiling and all the central floors collapsed, the marble columns rising from the edge of the abyss to support the charred, scalloped arches, the atmosphere dreamy with the smoke of one million Ottoman books gone up in flames. And now, in the midst of it all, I see my brother, intense and concentrated. The moon and the stars shine down on him and his orchestra. His arms are raised, the baton poised in his fingers. A flick, a spreading of the arms and the music soars up like a great voice from the heart of the earth. ❑

Ahdaf Souief's next novel, The Map of Love, *will be published by Bloomsbury Books in June*

PETER MORGAN

Bureaucracy of evil

Quietly and methodically the assets of murdered Jews were disposed of by the Nazis – only now are the records of those carefully ordered transactions coming to light

In the late summer of 1945, a young Jewish woman known as Marianne Stern arrived in Hemmerden, a small village near Cologne. According to the official report, Frau Stern had come back to reclaim family property seized by the Nazis in November 1941. She was the only member of her family to survive the concentration camps. Because her former home was now occupied by a German family, Frau Stern was forced to sleep in the cloisters of Hemmerden church. With the help of Herr Kruppel, a local tax officer, she recovered fragments of her past life: an ironing board, two dress cutting tables and her old sewing machine. Then, the document goes on, there was the matter of three family bicycles. Frau Stern asked the taxman to help her trace them; Herr Kruppel promised to come and see her. 'As he got closer,' she reports, 'I recognised his bike as that of my brother-in-law. He admitted this and, in April 1946, I got back my bike from him.'

Frau Stern's haunting story is drawn from a file in Cologne's wartime tax archive. Defying federal law, politics professor Dr Wolfgang Dressen recently put these documents on display in Dusseldorf's city museum. The exhibition was so popular – and provocative – that its run was extended by two months. For here, in one vast paper-chain, is the hidden history of the Holocaust. The buff files show how Jewish assets were systematically plundered and then sold off to German citizens at daily auctions.

'On page after page, you can see the commonplace cruelty of everyday life in Nazi Germany,' said Dressen. No items were too small for the clerk's ledger: an auction in Hemmerden ('held at 13-17

Hindenburgstrasse, 18 February 1942') lists the sale of frying pans, clothes hangers and even marmalade dishes. According to the inventory, six photos of the Jewish family in question remained unsold 'and were therefore sent away to be destroyed'. The tax officer organising these auctions was one Herr Kruppel.

Dr Dressen's research has revived the historical debate about how much ordinary Germans knew of the Holocaust. It's also highlighted another contemporary issue: what kind of details should be released about the recent past, and who should control access to such documents? In *The File*, Timothy Garton Ash likens Stasi files to 'poisoned madeleines': the Nazi tax files have the same power to unnerve and upset. Jewish claimants could use these detailed ledgers to trace confiscated family assets. They also provide an explicit account of

May 1933: Nazis collecting 'un-German' books and pamphlets thrown from a library's windows for destruction, with a band in attendance – Credit: Illustrated London News

individuals in Cologne who profited from the Holocaust. It's for this reason that the SPD (Social Democrat)-led government wants to keep the remaining files closed. Dr Dressen thinks that decision must be challenged in the German parliament and, if necessary, in the courts.

'The establishment tells us that to begin with, anti-semitism was an affair of extremes, that it was drunken and random,' he explained. 'But these files show that all levels of society were involved. In those auction records, you see items being bought by factory workers, the Protestant and Catholic Churches and even the town orphanage. It's all legal; it's all official; it's all normal. What you find in these files is criminality by legal means.'

Dressen, a serious and single-minded man, thinks there are around one million such files across Germany: a 'time bomb' of inventories, cargo manifests, auction sheets and restitution claims. 'It's important to realise that people bought these items in 1942 knowing that the Jews were not coming back,' he says. 'People knew what was happening, and so did the French and the Belgians. It's no secret. By the end of the war, almost every bombed family in Germany was sitting on stolen Jewish furniture.'

The exhibition is laid out in 12 'stations'; the penitential aspect of this display is thus made very clear. Examining the documents in their rectangular glass cases, it's surprising to learn that they are all photocopies. Over a nine month period, Dressen smuggled papers out of the Cologne archive, returning them the following day. 'When people ask how the documents got here, I always say it's by a kind of magic,' he says.

Each station examines a different stage in the confiscation process. The first concerns what was called *Vermogenserklarung*, the declaration of property. In October 1941, the German authorities ordered every Jewish family to draw up a list of its possessions. The lists retrieved by Dressen come in a range of shapes and sizes. Some are handwritten; some are typed. What they have in common is a devastating humanity; 'three bras, two pairs pants, two slips, one summer coat, one winter coat, one apron...' 'I started the exhibition with these documents because this is the last we see of these people,' says Dressen.

From November 1941, the official machine takes over. Station Two shows the typewritten deportation orders (*'Die Abschiebung von Juden...*) issued from Berlin. Stations Three and Four contain cargo manifests from the German train company, *Deutsche Reichsbahn*: 'one wagon-load of *Juden Mobiliar*', Jewish furniture, stamped, signed and countersigned. At each stage, Dressen shows how the confiscation was a very public affair: it was impossible not to have known what was going on. Station Five concerns the daily auctions in Cologne. On 22 July 1944, there was a sale of books 'from several Jews'. Among the job lot, a *History of the Renaissance* and the poems of Rilke. Dressen has also found letters from some of Germany's best known companies, each dealing matter of factly with stolen goods: Alianz, Dresdener Bank and Deutsche Bank are all represented here.

'The important point to stress is that in the eyes of these people, this was all legal and therefore entirely proper,' says Dr Dressen. 'As one woman in Hemmerden points out, "What the state does in our name cannot be unjust".' This legalistic, bureaucratic frame of mind continues well beyond the war. One of the last documents in the exhibition is dated 22 August 1945. Dusseldorf's *Oberfinanzprasident* compiles a restitution list, preparing to hand back to Jewish families the same assets he had confiscated four years earlier. 'Total cost of restitution: 117,714, 455 *Reich Marks*, and 26 *pfennigs*.'

Despite obstruction at a federal level, Dr Dressen has found some unexpected allies. The SPD-led governments in North-Rhine, Westphalia and Hessen have agreed to open up their archives, thus creating a useful precedent. 'In the long term, it's not possible for Bonn to forbid the publication of these archives,' he says, 'because two state governments have already opened the files.' Green MP Annalie Buntenbach supports this view. A respected campaigner against neo-Nazism, Buntenbach sees the tax files as a vital instument of political education. 'We have to have an honest discussion about the past, because only then can we stop new tendencies in the same direction,' she says. In the meantime, Dressen plans to take his exhibition on tour. Berlin is the next stop, though he would prefer somewhere more challenging. 'Berlin is very liberal, very thoughtful,' he says. 'But I would like to take it somewhere like Nuremberg or Munich. You know, somewhere that's very conservative and where it won't be liked. That would be a good provocation.' ❑

Peter Morgan is a reporter with Channel 4 News, UK

MICHAEL WALSH

The splendour of truth

'It is the first law of history not to say anything false,' wrote Pope Leo XIII upon opening the Vatican Archive to scholars for the first time in 1883, 'or to refrain from saying something which is true'

They look surprisingly attractive: long rows of leather-bound volumes on rows of shelving down enormous, dimly lit rooms which, I am assured by a senior archivist, are nuclear bomb-proof. These are the Secret Archives of the Vatican. Getting to them within the Vatican City is a touch daunting for the first-time visitor: permits (*tessere*), ID cards, close scrutiny by the mercenaries employed by the Pope to guard his territory, better known as the Swiss Guard.

'Secret'; however, turns out to be something of a misnomer, at least as usually understood. In English 'secret' means covert, hidden from view; in Latin or Italian it could just as easily mean separate, apart or, indeed, private. Which is what the documents preserved in the *Archivio Segreto* are: the private papers of popes and the Roman Curia.

The papacy has been around a long time; not quite as long as some of its apologists would have us believe, but long enough. By the middle of the seventh century, papal documents were being housed in the Lateran, the palace Emperor Constantine gave to the Pope as Bishop of Rome. They were frequently moved because the papacy in the Middle Ages was a good deal less sedentary than it has since become. In 1565, Pope Pius IV ordered the transfer of all papal documents from their several repositories to a new central archive in the Vatican. Paul V built what was to become the main part of the current archive in 1610, and the first consignment of papers arrived the following year.

And there they have stayed. Or mostly. There were problems when Rome, the last stronghold of the papal states, fell to the forces of united Italy in 1870, but the most significant disruption was Napoleon who, in 1809, ordered that the archives be transported to Paris. This took three years and 3,239 chests. When they were eventually returned after Napoleon's defeat, only 2,200 chests were needed. Some records never made it back and remain in Paris. Others were destroyed as being not worth the trouble of shipping. Yet more, in particular part of the archives of the Inquisition, were destroyed by the papal commissioners overseeing the transfer; some of these, rather circuitously, found their way to Trinity College, Dublin. Other chests were lost on the way to Rome when a boat sank on Lake Garda.

Until the last quarter of the nineteenth century these were not just the private archives of the papacy, to which non-current documents were transferred, but they were also secret in the usual sense of the word. It was not, in theory, possible to use them, but people were occasionally permitted to do so, either for particular projects or to make copies of documents relating to particular countries. Joseph Stevenson, a former employee of the British Museum turned Catholic priest, was sent to Rome in 1872 to copy, or have copied, papers of special interest to British historians. He was, for a time, given surprisingly free range of the archive's holdings and wandered more or less at will.

Leo XIII, who became Pope in 1878, decided the following year to open the archives to scholars. He did so, says Owen Chadwick in his fascinating volume on the opening of the Vatican Archives, *Catholicism and History*, because he wished to refute Italian anti-clericalism, which blamed the papacy for all Italy's ills. To Leo's immense satisfaction, the first volume of Ludwig Pastor's history of the papacy – which relied rather too heavily on quotations from the archives – demonstrated that, on the contrary, the papacy in the Renaissance had been at the centre of Italian culture. But when Pastor arrived at Alexander VI, without doubt the most dissolute of popes since the tenth century, at least one cardinal thought the third volume should be put on the *Index*. Leo XIII approved its publication nonetheless.

Would it were always so simple. The Archives have, like archives anywhere, a cut-off date. The Vatican's equivalent of the UK's '30-year rule' used to be that one could read papers produced in the last pontificate but eight; the present pope has reduced this to six.

Researchers can now consult papers up to the death, in 1922, of Pope Benedict XV. They cannot consult papers, therefore, produced in the pontificates of Pius XI, Pius XII, John XXIII, Paul VI, John Paul I or John Paul II. That prohibition extends to the war years but so incensed was the Vatican by charges against Pius XII over his treatment of the Jews that a special four-man team of Jesuits was commissioned to publish the *Actes et Documents du Saint Siège Relatifs à la Seconde Guerre Mondiale*. The 11 volumes appeared in 12 parts over 15 years.

They failed make the debate go away. Pierre Blet, the last of the four editors still alive, has vigorously defended the publication against those who claim significant papers were omitted. If they were, he has insisted, it was by accident not design, and any letter or other document which fell within the terms of the publication but was left out, ought to be published. Access to the war-year papers, however, will not be permitted to other scholars, according to the current regulations, until the death of the pope after next.

Even more restrictive rules apply to the papers of the Inquisition. In 1997 the Vatican announced that they were to be made available. There was great excitement, most of it misplaced. The Roman Inquisition was not as sanguinary as the Spanish one. As Dr Eamon Duffy of Magdalen College, Cambridge has pointed out, almost four times as many Protestants were put to death in England in three years by Mary Tudor as were executed in Italy under the Roman Inquisition in the whole of the sixteenth century. The latter had, of course, its *causes célèbres* – the burning of Giordano Bruno in Rome's Campo dei Fiore in 1600, for example, and the condemnation of Galileo in 1616 and 1632. For much of its existence, however, the Roman Inquisition was concerned with the maintenance of order in the Papal States – something of interest to Italian historians undoubtedly, but less so to historians of the Church.

Until, that is, 1903. In that year Pius X – since declared to be a saint – became pope and soon afterwards began a campaign against Modernism. This movement had its eccentricities but, in essence, it was an attempt to reconcile contemporary scholarship with the Bible and the history of Catholic doctrine. The persecution of those suspected of Modernism was intense, unjust and, from the perspective of the present, plain wrong. The condemnations issued by the Biblical Commission against certain interpretations of the Scriptures, have all since been swept away. But they were issued with the greatest confidence with the authority of St Pius himself, and they touched a great many scholars, including the future Pope John XXIII.

The 27 rooms and the circa 7,000 volumes of the Inquisition have been opened to researchers. There alone, disgracefully, the old rules of 'eight popes back' still applies. Papers are available not to 1922, but to 1903 before the serious persecution of Modernists began. Pastor once heard Leo XIII say 'the church rejoices in the splendour of the truth'. As that trenchantly conservative Catholic Evelyn Waugh might have said: 'Up to a point, Cardinal Copper.' ❏

Michael Walsh is librarian of Heythrop College, University of London, which specialises in philosophy and theology. He has written a number of books, including a study of the secretive Catholic organisation Opus Dei, and a biography of the present Pope

Credit: Erica Baum/D'Amelio Terras Gallery, New York

IAGUBA DIALLO

Suddenly last summer

A nation can lose its memory in one fell swoop as the West African state of Guinea-Bissau discovered in June last year

The war which flared up in Guinea-Bissau on 7 June last year between the military junta – representing 90 per cent of the armed forces – reinforced by veterans of the armed struggle for national liberation, and the remaining 10 per cent who supported relief troops from Senegal and Guinea-Conakry solicited by President Joao Bernardo Vieira, exerted a heavy toll, even if the precise details remain unclear.

To the unknown number of deaths can be added some 250,000 displaced persons and refugees, and the enormous material destruction caused by intense bombardment with heavy artillery during 50 days of confrontation. Among the structures worst affected was the National Institute of Studies and Research (INEP), the largest and most active research institution in the tiny country. The complex housing INEP is located less than a kilometre from the front-line. It was transformed into an advance post for Senegalese troops. The later transformation of the three-floor complex into an army barracks and the subsequent bombardments, caused immense damages.

Thanks to the ceasefire signed on 25 August, a few staff members were authorised, after enormous difficulties, to visit their former place of work. The preliminary balance-sheet can be summarised in one word: disastrous. All the workrooms were forcibly opened, emptied of their contents and transformed into dormitories; documents were thrown outside and left exposed to the elements. Dozens of computers containing databases on all aspects of life in Guinea-Bissau, compiled painstakingly during the last 15 years, have disappeared. Those left behind were cannibalised.

Sensitive and very rare equipment, such as the only digital cartography table in the country, was jettisoned outside. The INEP Library, embryo of the National Library and a reference centre for all publications, is roofless, its walls damaged. The torrential rains which have fallen on Bissau since the end of June constantly enter the building. Its three floors have been transformed into pools where thousands of books and journals float.

The library contained around 60,000 books, 1,000 periodical titles, 2,000 microfiches and countless discs, an essential national database. All these materials were scattered, shredded and exposed to the rain and dirt, along with the bulk of the National Archives stored in the building. The hundreds of audio cassettes, which record the history of the national liberation struggle as told by its actors and witnesses, as well as others containing an oral history of the different regions, have disappeared.

Photographs and films from the audio-visual archives are found dispersed and lying in the mud outside. In other words, entire pages of the history of Guinea-Bissau risk being irredeemably blank, or illegible. This is particularly serious in view of the fact that no general history of the country has yet been written, and that all recent efforts by the Institute had been geared toward this objective. The damage suffered by INEP has reduced to zero the enormous efforts made since independence to provide a centre of documentation and research useful to all those interested in Guinea-Bissau.

At the time of writing, INEP continues to be a military camp, in spite of the ceasefire. The staff are forbidden to engage in work to rehabilitate or save it from further destruction. Relentlessly, the disaster continues. This letter to inform is also an SOS for the largest research institution of Guinea-Bissau, now threatened with extinction. I urge you to forward this message to all friends of INEP, as well as to all institutions and individuals who attach value to intellectual production. ❏

Iaguba Diallo is director of Guinea Bissau's National Institute of Studies and Research (INEP). This edited letter was circulated in September. A transitional government, composed of both sides in the conflict, was sworn in on 20 February this year and the withdrawal of 3,000 troops from Senegal and Guinea has begun. They are due to be replaced by troops from Niger and Bénin prior to fresh elections later this year

word power

from *The Love of a Good Woman*, Alice Munro

The other thing I did behind the curtain was read. I read books that I got from the Kitsilano Library a few blocks away. And when I looked up in that churned up state of astonishment that a book could bring me to, a giddiness of gulped riches, the stripes were what I'd see. And not just the characters, the story, but the climate of the book became attached to the unnatural flowers and flowed along in the dark-wine stream or the gloomy green. I read the heavy books whose titles were already familiar and incantatory to me – I even tried to read the novels of Aldous Huxley and Henry Green, and *To the Lighthouse* and *The Last of Chéri* and *The Death of the Heart*. I bolted them down one after the other without establishing any preferences, surrendering to each in turn just as I'd done to the books I read in my childhood. I was still in that stage of leaping appetite, of voracity close to anguish.

But one complication had been added since childhood – it seemed that I had to be a writer as well as a reader. I bought a school notebook and tried to write – did write, pages that started off authoritatively and then went dry, so that I had to tear them out and twist them up in hard punishment and put them in the garbage can. I did this over and over again until I had only the notebook cover left. Then I bought another notebook and started the whole process once more. The same cycle – excitement and despair, excitement and despair. It was like having a secret pregnancy and miscarriage every week. ❏

NADINE GORDIMER

Morning in the library: 1975

Its battles for racial and ideological purity left apartheid South Africa one of the most censored nations on earth

R ecently I spent a strange morning in a library.

It was the reference section of the Johannesburg Municipal Library; I had entered, made my request to a solicitously attentive librarian, followed her to a glass-fronted case, waited while she unlocked it and removed a large, loose-leafed volume for me.

Now I sat down with the other users of the library at one of the drawing room-glossy tables. It was good to find myself among people of all colours, absorbed in their reading; faded and ridiculous, those days not long ago, when to work here and take advantage of the courteous and knowledgeable help of the librarians whites kept for themselves. A crumbling at the edges of the apartheid fortress had at least taken place. Now all my fellow Johannesburgers were surrounded by books. Some had piled a lair against distraction; some stared at an array set out like a hand of patience. A young girl opposite me was making notes, hovering from source to source above spread volumes. Quietly, with the creaking of boots or the lisp of crêpe rubber, the offices of this temple of learning were performed as people went back and forth between the shelves, taking and replacing books, more books.

I alone had only one before me. It occupied me the whole morning; it was, in a sense, the Book of Books, whose word is set up against that of all others. My book was *Jacobsen's Index of Objectionable Literature*, the bible of South African censorship. And so, while the search for knowledge, know-how, spiritual enlightenment and the pleasures of poetry went on about me – like most writers, I am as practiced a squinter as I am an eavesdropper, and I noted Wittgenstein, *Teach Yourself Accountancy*, Pascal's *Pensées*, Seventeenth Century English Verse – I read on down the lists of banned books in Jacobsen.

There is a great deal of trash, of course. Paperbacks of the kind that are twirled round on wire stands in chewing-gum-and-smokes shops and airports; the titles of the banned ones don't sound any different from those I see on sale everywhere. The sheer volume of sub-literature swamps the resources of censorship in that category. And there are books I suppose we could be said to be lucky to do without? Dr Rubin never gets a chance to tell us *Everything We Always Wanted To Know About Sex And Were Afraid To Ask*.

The 'highest literary judgement' South Africans are constantly assured is a qualification of the government-appointed censors, who consider literature, plays and films, apparently is just as good for extra-literary purposes: the censors are expected to bring this judgment to bear upon, and indeed have banned, T-shirts bearing saucy legends, a black fist and even the peace sign. Let us not bother to recall the famous pantyhose packet; there was also a glass that, on being filled with liquid, showed the figure of a nude woman. There they are, listed in Jacobsen.

But it's easy to laugh at the South African censors. Our amusement, their solemn ridiculousness – these have not undermined their power. Indeed, as we know, the renewed and tightened censorship legislation (it was first imposed in the 1960s) that came into force on 1 April this year [1975] protects the newly-chosen personnel both from ridicule and from exposure should their decisions be challenged. The right of appeal to a court of law against bannings has been taken from writers and it is now an offence against the law to criticise members of the Special Appeals Board set up within the censorship organisation to hear appeals against decisions made by its own regional censorship committees.

Most titles my finger was running down, page after page, were banned by the Publications Control Board before April. They constitute virtually the entire *oeuvre* of black South African fiction writers, essayists and some poets, including Lewis Nkosi, Alex la Guma, Ezekiel Mphahlele and Denis Brutus, and individual works by myself, Jack Cope, Mary Benson, C J Driver, André Brink and others, black and white.

Bans on British, US and European writers include works by Kingsley

Amis, Vladimir Nabokov, Bernard Malamud, Norman Mailer, John O'Hara, John Masters, James Baldwin, Edna O'Brien, John Updike, Frederic Raphael, Joseph Heller, Robert Penn Warren, Gore Vidal, Han Suyin, James Purdy, William Burroughs, Erica Jong, Langston Hughes, Doris Lessing, Paul Theroux, Truman Capote, Allan Sillitoe, Sinclair Lewis, William Styron, Alison Lurie, Phillip Roth, Jakov Lind, J P Donleavy, Kurt Vonnegut and Jack Kerouac. Translations include books by Joseph Kessel, Jean-Paul Sartre, Romain Gary, Alberto Moravia, Carlos Fuentes, Roger Peyrefitte, Jean Genet, Françoise Mallet-Joris, Junichiro Tanazaki, Alain Robbe-Grillet, Colette, Nikos Kazantzakis, Jean Cocteau, Alfred Jarry, Vasco Pratolini, Vladimir Mayakovsky, Marguerite Duras, Guy de Maupassant and Pierre Louys.

Among contemporary thinkers there are works by Herbert Marcuse, Oscar Lewis, Salvador Allende, Wilhelm Reich, Louis Althusser and Lezek Kolakowski.

Some of the bannings of the new censorship organisation were too recent yet to have found their place in Jacobsen's *Index*. Iris Murdoch 's *The Black Prince* was one. Wopko Jensma's *Where White is the Colour, Black is the Number*, Mary Benson's *The Sun Will Rise* and Breyten Breytenbach's latest work, were others. And the day after I spent my morning in the library reading about what we may not read, our new and greatly enlarged team of censors showed nothing if not extraordinary breadth of literary judgment – at one eclectic stroke they banned George Lukacs's *History and Class Consciousness* and 13 pairs of men's underpants bearing legends such as 'Long John Silver'.

If you don't believe me, you can go to our library and look it all up in the Book of Books. ❏

Nadine Gordimer was the winner of the Nobel prize in 1991. Her latest novel is The House Gun (Bloomsbury). *The above essay will appear in the forthcoming* Living in Hope and History: Notes From Our Century, *a personal selection of her non-fiction writing, to appear towards the end of 1999*

*A Full and True Account of the
BATTLE Fought last FRIDAY, Between
the Ancient and the Modern BOOKS
in St. JAMES's LIBRARY*, Swift

The guardian of the regal library, a person of great valour but chiefly renowned for his *humanity, had been a fierce champion for the Moderns; and, in an engagement upon Parnassus, had vowed, with his own hands, to knock down two of the Ancient chiefs who guarded a small pass on the superior rock; but endeavouring to climb up was cruelly obstructed by his own unhappy weight and tendency towards the centre, a quality to which those of the Modern party are extreme subject; for, being light-headed, they have in speculation a wonderful agility, and conceive nothing too high for them to mount; but in reducing to practice, discover a mighty pressure about the posteriors and their heels. Having thus failed in his design, the disappointed champion bore a cruel rancour to the Ancients, which he resolved to gratify by showing all marks of his favour to the books of their adversaries, and lodging them in the fairest apartments when at the same time, whatever book had the boldness to own itself for an advocate of the Ancients, was buried alive in some obscure corner, and threatened upon the least displeasure to be turned out of doors. Besides, it so happened that about this time there was a strange confusion of place among all the books in the library, for which several reasons were assigned. Some imputed it to a great heap of learned dust, which a perverse wind blew off from a shelf of Moderns into the keeper's eyes. Others affirmed he had a humour to pick the worms out of the schoolmen, and swallow them fresh and fasting; whereof some fell upon his spleen, and some climbed up into his head, to the great perturbation of both. And lastly, others maintained that by walking much in the dark about the library, he had quite lost the situation of it out of his head; and therefore, in replacing his books, he was apt to mistake and clap Déscartes next to Aristotle; poor Plato had got between Hobbes and *Seven Wise Masters*, and Virgil was hemmed in with Dryden on one side, and Withers on the other.

* The Honourable Mr. Boyle, in the preface to his edition of *Phalaris*, says he was refused a manuscript by the library-keeper, *'pro solita humanitate suâ'*.

MICHAEL FOLEY

Marsh's Library

In 1701 Dublin was a 'lewd and debauched' town with nowhere to sit down and read. Archbishop Marsh's gift remedied at least the second complaint

Just past Dublin's St Patrick's Cathedral, where Jonathan Swift was once dean, and down a little curved street, there is a door in a high brick wall. Inside, steps lead to a door. Enter beneath the portal marked 'Marsh's Library' and, as if by some freak of time travel, you are transported back to the Dublin of the eighteenth century.

Marsh's is the oldest public library in Ireland, arguably the oldest in Britain, too. Founded in 1701 by Archbishop Narcissus Marsh, 20 years after he first arrived in Dublin as Provost of Trinity College in 1679 and discovered there was nowhere in the city where the public could go to read, his library was a surprising gift, perhaps, to a city he called 'this lewd and debauched town'.

The library, a magnificent example of a seventeenth-century scholar's library, has hardly changed in 300 years. Its two long galleries of tall oak bookcases, each beneath a carved and lettered gable and topped with a mitre, lead to three gated alcoves in which readers with particularly valuable books were caged in. Swift may well have sat here facing the skull across the desk as he worked on *Gulliver's Travels* or made his notes in the margins of the books he studied; the library has a copy of Clarendon's *History of the Rebellion*, extensively annotated in the dean's hand.

The library houses four main collections from the sixteenth, seventeenth and early-eighteenth centuries. There are many liturgical works, Bibles printed in almost every language and books relating to the religious controversies of their day.

With the exception of his Oriental collection, which is in Oxford's Bodleian Library, Marsh left his own books to his library. He was a man

Marsh's alcoves – Credit: Marsh's Library

with wide-ranging interests in science and mathematics and many of the works are annotated by him. He also collected books in Hebrew, Arabic, Turkish and Russian.

He also purchased the libraries of others, from the likes of Edward Stillingfleet (1635-99), Bishop of Worcester, for instance. Marsh bought his library of nearly 10,000 books for £2,500 in 1705. Such collectors were men with scholarly tastes and the library reflects their broad interests. The collection houses works on medicine, law, science, travel, navigation, mathematics, music and classical literature. As one walks through the library there is a sense of being surrounded by the great debates and controversies of the seventeenth century, as well as by the science, the inventions and the sheer curiosity that characterised the European Enlightenment.

Though it does house an important collection of printed books and periodicals relating to Irish history from the past century, Marsh's is not a narrowly Irish library but a library of European significance, of European thought. Indeed, its first librarian was not an Irishman, but a Huguenot refugee, Dr Elias Bouhéreau, who fled persecution in France following the revocation of the Edict of Nantes in 1685. His own collection of Protestant theology and polemic is still in the library.

The present librarian, Muriel McCarthy, is the first woman to hold the position. It is she who welcomes the governors and guardians to the library for their annual visitation every second Thursday in October, as they have done for the past 300 years. Like Dean Swift, the dean of Christchurch Cathedral is an *ex officio* governor.

In addition to the collections, there are a number of significant individual items: a small book of Elizabethan poetry with a poem to Queen Elizabeth by Sir Walter Raleigh; two volumes of the first Irish-language Bible in Bishop Bedell's original translation; and of course, a Joyce connection. A copy of the first US edition of *Ulysses,* published when the book was still banned in Britain and Ireland, sits beside a mediaeval work by the Abbot Joachim of Flora, a book Joyce went to Marsh's to consult on 22 and 23 October 1902 having seen a reference to Joachim in a short story by Yeats. 'Come out of them, Stephen,' he later wrote in *Ulysses.* 'Beauty is not there. Nor in the stagnant bay of Marsh's library where you read the fading prophecies of Joachim Abbas.'

But the ghost of Narcissus Marsh cannot leave his library. He still paces the shelves looking, it is said, for a letter from his niece. She eloped from his house next door with a clergyman and married him at Castleknock, outside Dublin. The letter, hidden in one of the books, is, Ms McCarthy tells schoolchildren, her expression of regret. ❏

Michael Foley *is a lecturer in journalism at the Dublin Institute of Technology*

JOHN MEDCALF

Barefoot messengers

'Senores bibliotecarios, I am a simple illiterate woman but, thanks to one of your books, I have learned to make trousers and shirts. The men used to buy their clothes from a village called Hong Kong, but now they buy them from me.'

The Rural Library Network in northern Peru was inspired by a 12-year-old boy. In 1972, I was the new priest of the isolated and poverty-stricken parish of Bambamarca. Twenty thousand peasant families eked a living from maize and potatoes harvested at heights of up to 12,000 feet above sea level.

One wet afternoon a poncho-clad boy came to my office.

'Padre, our teacher says you have books.'

'Well of course I have books.'

'But I've never seen a book and I want to.'

'Well how did you learn to read without books?'

Leonardo Herrera then described how the teacher had a minuscule blackboard, and how the pupils would cut a cactus leaf on which they would carve letters and numbers with a nail, a key or a knife. So I selected from my book shelf a history of Peru written in Spanish and handed it to Leonardo. 'I will lend this to you for a week, Leo. Then perhaps I'll lend you another book if you've looked after this one.'

Shortly before the dawn of the next day, I was woken by knocking of MacDuffian insistence. Expecting a sick-call, I confronted Leonardo instead.

'I've finished the book!' he shouted triumphantly.

'You can't have done. There's no electricity in your village.'

'Oh, I borrowed a few candles from your church.'

The lad had sat up reading all night. He had even made spidery notes on paper I had given him and he wanted the second volume of the history of Peru.

Three decades later there are nearly 600 village libraries spread over the length of this mountainous country. The three principal influences on the network are the pedagogy of Paulo Freire, the barefoot doctors of China and the British public library system. Freire taught that literacy programmes were pointless without the availability of suitable reading materials; China warned us against vehicles, which would be difficult and expensive to maintain (we refused several offers of 'bibliobuses'); the British system encouraged us to give readers direct access to books (not just to a filing cabinet) and to adapt the Dewey System to our very special requirements.

The earliest rural libraries were attached to village schools, but when teachers failed to cooperate, village elders took over control. Librarians were proposed and el;ected by a show of hands. In addition to monthly visits to Cajamarca City to exchange the books, librarians took on responsibility for all cultural activities and even the protection of archaeological sites from marauders and tomb-robbers.

After a few years of modest success, a conservative mayor (who was also a big landowner) approached me one day: 'Padre, what's so special about books? Why don't we put a television in every village instead?' His intentions were obvious. Books were subversive, awakening the minds of the *campesinos*. Television – especially the *Dallas* and *Dynasty* type of programmes to which we were then subjected – would quickly numb any tendency to creative thinking.

Our barefoot librarians walk up to 15 hours a day with a knapsack or – if they are lucky enough to have a pack animal – with a saddle-bag. These contain an average of 24 books. A typical selection would include books on health and first aid (*Where There is No Doctor* is a favourite); history; children's stories (which are read by adults as well, making up for lost infancies); legislation (surprisingly popular, especially where the defence of their own interests is concerned); poetry, legends and folk-tales; a religious book or two; and perhaps a book about cooperatives and current affairs.

In recent years, my successor, Alfredo Mires, has encouraged the writing and publication of books by the peasant librarians and their readers. These illustrated books have proven to be enormously popular. After all, reading and writing (like charity) begin at home.

We were at a coordinators' meeting one day when a *campesina* woman interrupted us. '*Senores bibliotecarios*, I am a simple illiterate woman but, thanks to one of your books, I have learned to make trousers and shirts. The men used to buy their clothes from a village called Hong Kong, but now they buy them from me.' Her children, who went to the village school, were able to read to the mother the text that accompanied the drawings.

Once we linked up with the Technical University of Cajamarca, when villagers requested practical help with bee-keeping. The students were amazed at how proficient the *campesinos* had become thanks to books on agriculture published in Argentina and Uruguay.

The libraries continue to grow, in spite of government indifference and, in the past, open hostility. The network provides a cheap imitable model of adult education. Peasant families are encouraged not to migrate to the big cities. Leonardo is now a village schoolteacher, but libraries are still his first love. Like MacDuff, he knocked – and was answered. ❏

John Medcalf spent 30 years as a priest in south and central America, founding the Rural Library Network in Peru in 1971. He is currently chairman of the Peru Support Group (PSG). Donations to the libraries may be sent to 122 Ladbroke Road, Redhill, Surrey, RH1 1LF. For further information about Peru, call PSG at 0171-620-1103.

WOLE SOYINKA

Two Poems for the Pen

AH, DEMOSTHENES!

I shall ram pebbles in my mouth
Demosthenes
Not to choke, but half-dolphin, half
Shark hammer-head from fathoms deep
ride the waves to charge the breakers
They erect.
Crush impediment of power and inundate
Their tainted towers-
I shall ram pebbles in my mouth.

I shall place nettles on my tongue
Demosthenes
Then thwart its stung retraction. Oh,
Let it burn at root and roof
Let rashes break from every pore
Just so it sear the tyrant's power
With one response
I shall place nettles on my tongue.

But have you heard of *werepe*
Demosthenes?
Not all your Stoics' calm can douse
The fiery hairs of that infernal pod.
It makes a queen run naked to the world
An itch that tells the world its flesh
Is whorish sick
I shall place *werepe* on every tongue.

I'll drop some ratsbane on my tongue
Demosthenes
To bait the rodents with a kiss of death
I'll seal their fate in tunnels dark and dank
As habitations of their hostages
Denied of air, denied of that same light
Their hands had cupped to immerse their world
I'll drop some ratsbane on my tongue

I'll thrust all fingers down the throat
Demosthenes
To raise a spout of bile to drown the world.
It's petrified, Demosthenes, mere forms,
Usurp the hearts we knew, mere rasps.
This stuttering does not become the world.
This tongue of millions fugitive from truth
I'll thrust all fingers down the throat.

I'll let the hemlock pass
Demosthenes –
Oh, not between my lips – I've shared
Its thin dissolve in myriad throats
At one with that agnostic sage.
They did not stutter like the world they left –
And I know why –
Their lives were spent with heated pebbles
On their tongues, Demosthenes!

PENS FOR HIRE

The pen may beat a path to ploughshares
Pen beat ploughshares into swords
In words from ploughshare and the sword.
And pen enshrine and pen unmask the lies
Of vain mythologies, pen enthrone
The mouldy claims of Power, urge
Contested spaces as divinely given.

Pen prove mighty ear of swords
Glory tongue of gory deeds, dress rape
In fame, plunder in time-honoured robes
Of epic deeds. The pen may dip
In ink-well and emerging,
Drip with blood.

Precious stones adorn their tongues of note,
Of cant of sterile incantation.
Show me the water beds they lie upon
Pull the plug and puzzle why the flow is darkened red
and thick, and clotted. Eternally

In swarm as locusts, as lies and flies, consorts
Drawn to dark orgies of commemorating pens –

Long is the line of great seductions
Lure of ease within our chequered tribe – from griots
Of voice, to plume, and the compact processor,
Some, we have come to know. They served
And were served in turn. Some believed,
And others cashed their souls in make-believe.

But both are immunised against the testament
Of eyes, and ears, the stench and guilt of power
And anomy of reddening rain, of plagues of locusts.
Deaths of firstborns, seven lean years and
Yet again the eighth and sequent round
 Of death and dearth. A pledge not earned or given
Is not in mortals to redeem.

But God decreed the end shall multiply the means -
A seasoned waiter, the pen inscribes:
We also serve. ❑

Wole Soyinka *is Nigeria's foremost writer and poet. In 1986 he became the first African to win the Nobel Prize for Literature.*

word power

from *The Library of Babel*, Jorge Luís Borges
translated by Andrew Hurley

When it was announced that the Library contained all books, the first reaction was unbounded joy. All men felt themselves the possessors of an intact and secret treasure. There was no personal problem, no world problem, whose eloquent solution did not exist – somewhere in that hexagon. The universe was justified; the universe suddenly became congruent with the unlimited width and breadth of mankind's hope. At the same period there was also hope that the fundamental mysteries of mankind – the origin of the Library and of time – might be revealed. In all likelihood those profound mysteries can indeed be explained in words; if the language of the philosophers is not sufficient, then the multiform Library must surely have produced the extraordinary language that is required, together with the words and grammar of that language. For four centuries, men have been scouring the hexagons. There are official searchers, the 'inquisitors'. I have seen them about their tasks: they arrive exhausted at some hexagon, they talk about a staircase that nearly killed them – rungs were missing – they speak with the librarian about galleries and staircases, and, once in a while, they take up the nearest book and leaf through it, searching for disgraceful or dishonourable words. Clearly no one expects to discover anything.

That unbridled hopefulness was succeeded, naturally enough, by a similarly disproportionate depression. The certainty that some bookshelf in some hexagon contained precious books, yet that those precious books were forever out of reach, was almost unbearable. One blasphemous sect proposed that the searches be discontinued and that all men shuffle letters and symbols until those canonical books, through some improbable stroke of chance, had been constructed.

Others, going about it in the opposite way, thought the first thing to do was eliminate all worthless books. They would invade the hexagons, leaf disgustedly through a volume, and condemn entire walls of books. It is to their hygienic, ascetic rage that we lay the loss of millions of volumes. Their name is execrated today, but those who grieve over the 'treasures' destroyed overlook two widely acknowledged facts: one, that the Library is so huge that any reduction by human hands must be infinitesimal. And two, that each book is unique and irreplaceable, but (since the Library is total) there are always several hundred thousand imperfect facsimiles – books that differ by no more than a single letter, or a comma. ❏

Raw copy

This column is usually reserved for calm, sometimes ironic, speculation concerning the antics of the media, with reference to contiguous incidents of the abuse of freedom of expression culled from the pages of the section that follows, *Index Index*. This 27-year-old archive of censorship from around the world mingles terse reports of the murder of journalists in Latin America and Russia, with the newest legal eccentricities from the First Amendment battlefield in the US and the campaigns by Balkan minorities for linguistic or political freedoms.

The raw copy from which *Index Index* is distilled is consistently twice the length of the finished product and cutting it requires a cautious balancing of priorities. Is the death of a journalist in a country like Colombia – which produces a hearty crop of them each year – more worthy of space than a potentially landmark court decision on internet freedoms? Does the banning of the lesbian-themed film *Fire*, say more about the state of expressive freedoms in India than the burning to death of a Christian missionary and his two young sons? *Index Index* tries to solve this dilemma by printing episodes which demonstrate the expanding nature of censorship, while continuing to 'witness' to those who have died in the course of their work.

This edition was different from its predecessors. There was such an avalanche of raw censorship material that it could not be cut to fit the demands of the section without doing a grave disservice to the people concerned. With UK Foreign Secretary Robin Cook and the press preoccupied with the 'Arms to Sierra Leone' row, it was easy to forget that ordinary people suffer far more than politicians from the illegal export of weapons. In Sierra Leone, rebel Revolutionary United Front (RUF) appeared to have targeted media workers for elimination and, in January, the country lost almost as many journalists as Colombia in a whole year.

Jenner Cole of SKY-FM, **Mohammed Kamara** of KISS-FM and **Paul Mansaray**, deputy editor of the newspaper *Standard Times* were killed on 9 January. Cole was abducted by rebels from his Freetown

Simon Davies on

PRIVACY

Patricia Williams on

RACE

Gabriel Garcia Marquez on

JOURNALISM

Edward Lucie-Smith on

THE INTERNET

Ursula Owen on

HATE SPEECH

...all in INDEX

SUBSCRIBE & SAVE

UK and overseas

○ **Yes! I want to subscribe to *Index*.**

❐ 1 year (6 issues)   £39   Save 28%
❐ 2 years (12 issues)   £74   Save 31%
❐ 3 years (18 issues)   £102   **You save 37%**

Name

Address

                                                                    B9B2

£ _____ enclosed. ❏ Cheque (£) ❏ Visa/MC ❏ Am Ex ❏ Bill me
(Outside of the UK, add £6 a year for foreign postage)

Card No.

Expiry   Signature

❏ I do not wish to receive mail from other companies.

INDEX ON CENSORSHIP

✉ Freepost: INDEX, 33 Islington High Street, London N1 9BR
☎ (44) 171 278 2313 Fax: (44) 171 278 1878
e tony@indexoncensorship.org

SUBSCRIBE & SAVE

North America

○ **Yes! I want to subscribe to *Index*.**

❐ 1 year (6 issues) $52   Save 21%
❐ 2 years (12 issues) $96   Save 27%
❐ 3 years (18 issues) $135   **You save 32%**

Name

Address

                                                                    B9B3

$ _____ enclosed. ❏ Cheque ($) ❏ Visa/MC ❏ Am Ex ❏ Bill me

Card No.

Expiry   Signature

❏ I do not wish to receive mail from other companies.

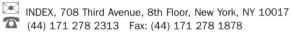

INDEX ON CENSORSHIP

✉ INDEX, 708 Third Avenue, 8th Floor, New York, NY 10017
☎ (44) 171 278 2313 Fax: (44) 171 278 1878
e tony@indexoncensorship.org

home and was being taken to a Revolutionary United Front (RUF) base when, after some disruption caused by ECOMOG, he was summarily shot in the head in front of his fiancée. Kamara was similarly seized in his home and questioned. When the rebels were satisfied he was the journalist they were seeking, they shot him dead. Paul Mansaray was murdered at home in Freetown, along with his wife, two young children and a nephew. A fellow journalist, who alerted Mansaray when he saw RUF soldiers approaching, sought refuge in a neighbour's house and overheard the rebels threatening Mansaray because of his work. The rebels set Mansaray's house ablaze and sprayed it with gunfire, with Mansaray and his family inside.

Missing but feared dead were **Michael Charlie Hinga**, a broadcaster for the Sierra Leone Broadcasting Service (SLBS), **Mabay Kamara**, a freelance reporter and **James Ogogo**, an editorial consultant for *Concord Times*. Kamara was abducted by rebels from his Freetown house, which was then set on fire. His wife, who witnessed the abduction, has also disappeared. Ogogo, a Nigerian, was feared to have been captured by the RUF while fleeing to a safer area of the capital. The only journalist reported to have survived a direct physical attack by RUF forces to date is **Mustapha Sesay**, a production manager for *Standard Time*. He was attacked by rebels armed with cutlasses who gouged out his right eye with a machete. Voice of America stringer **Kelvin Lewis**' house was burned down by the rebels, but he managed to escape while carrying his 70-year-old mother in his arms.

Munir Turay, a freelance journalist for the independent newspaper *Punch* and state-owned newspaper *Daily Mail*, was also killed between 9 and 15 January in Kissy, east Freetown. Neither his family nor his colleagues know the exact circumstances of his death but his body had bullet holes on the back. **Abdulai Juma Jalloh**, news editor of the independent *African Champion*, was killed by an ECOMOG soldier in Central Freetown. He had been accused of resembling someone who owed a civil defence officer money and was later told he had been identified as a rebel. He denied the accusations but was taken aside and executed at point-blank range in front of his editor, Mohammed D. Koroma. ❏

MG

A censorship chronicle incorporating information from the American Association for the Advancement of Science Human Rights Action Network (AAASHRAN), Amnesty International (AI), Article 19 (A19), the BBC Monitoring Service Summary of World Broadcasts (SWB), the Committee to Protect Journalists (CPJ), the Canadian Committee to Protect Journalists (CCPJ), the Inter-American Press Association (IAPA), the International Federation of Journalists (IFJ/FIP), the International Federation of Newspaper Publishers (FIEJ), Human Rights Watch (HRW), the Media Institute of Southern Africa (MISA), International PEN (PEN), Open Media Research Institute (OMRI), Reporters Sans Frontières (RSF), the World Association of Community Broadcasters (AMARC), the World Organisation Against Torture (OMCT) and other sources

ANGOLA

On 11 January the authorities arrested two journalists from the independent Radio Morena in Benguela. Director **José Manuel Alberto** and administrator **José Cabral Sande** were picked up by intelligence officers shortly after the station rebroadcast a bulletin from Radio Televisão Portuges (RTP) which said that rebel UNITA forces had taken control of Vila Nova in the province of Huambo. They were held at a local police station for 'disobedience and offences against the head of state'. (MISA)

ARGENTINA

On 11 December four officers

of the air force received suspensions of eight to 30 days for spying on 10 journalists. According to the head of Department III of Central Office Intelligence, Jorge Alberto Lopez, the journalists were suspected of serving 'foreign interests'. (Periodistas)

Carlos Alberto Vila Ortiz, a 63-year-old writer and journalist, was attacked at his doorway on 29 December. Vila had stepped out in response to a knock on his window. Once outside, two men plunged a screw into his scrotum before being scared off by security guards. In 1994 Vila was forced to abandon the managing editorship of the daily *La Capital* after his grandchildren were threatened at gunpoint. (Periodistas)

Bernardo Balbuena, editor of the daily *El Diario de Resistencia*, was attacked by unidentified individuals on 5 January. The assailants jumped over a two-metre high security fence, broke into the journalist's home and and damaged his car. The newspaper had recently published reports about the corruption of Raul Romero Feris, mayor of Corrientes and owner of the daily *Norte de Resistencia*. (Periodistas)

On 25 January journalistic associations commemorated the second anniversary of the assassination of **José Luís Cabezas**, photographer for *Noticias* magazine (*Index* 2/1997, 3/1997, 5/1997). The investigation was closed in December 1998 and the trial is slated for May. The judge leading the investigations, Jude

Macchi, has been criticised for procedural errors and being unable to identify either the authors or the motive of the crime. (RSF, Periodistas)

ARMENIA

The Yerevan newspaper *Oragir* opened a lawsuit against Interior and National Security Minister Serzh Sarkisian, a key ally of President Kocharian, for defamation on 6 February. On 30 January Sarkisian told another newspaper that 'everything published in *Oragir* is slander'. (RFE/RL)

Recent publication: *Comments on the Initial Report Submitted to the United Nations Human Rights Committee* (AI, September 1998, 17pp)

AUSTRALIA

In late November Stephen Walsh, a Palm Island councillor, called on citizens to boycott the 45th edition of the *Guinness Book of World Records* for describing the remote Aboriginal island as 'the most violent place on earth outside a combat zone'. (*Daily Telegraph*)

AZERBAIJAN

Azadliq newspaper and its editor, **Gunduz Tahirli**, were fined 500 million manat (US$130,000) after they were convicted by Baku City Court of 'insulting the honour' of 14 state officials by printing details of the property they owned abroad. Among the plaintiffs was Djalal Aliyev, brother of the president (*Index* 1/1999). (Azerbaijani Journalists' Trade Union)

Ayna correspondent **Azer Rashidoglu** was beaten by a security officer of the Milli Mejlis (National Assembly) on 22 December, as he attempted to report the assembly's proceedings. Journalists were beaten 108 times in 1998. The opposition newspapers *Yeni Musavat* and *Azadliq* were the riskiest places to work, with their reporters harassed or assaulted 17 and 15 times respectively. The unluckiest individual was freelance journalist **Ibrahim Niyazli**, who was beaten three times and had his house repossessed. (Azerbaijani Journalists' Trade Union)

Yalchin Imanov, a correspondent for *Yeni Musavat* newspaper, was beaten by the mayor of Barda's bodyguard as he arrived for a pre-arranged interview with the mayor on 3 January. *Yeni Musavat* editor Rauf Arifoglu said Imanov was then taken to the Barda police station where he was beaten and detained overnight. (Azerbaijan National Democracy Foundation, Human Rights Centre of Azerbaijan)

Azadliq journalist **Hadji Zamin**, who had written critically about the abuse of power in the army, received papers on 6 January drafting him for military service. (Human Rights Centre of Azerbaijan)

On 12 January *525 Gazet* reported complaints from Jehovah's Witnesses that they had been subject to persecution and pressure, and their books had been confiscated by the police. It cited Mustafa Ibrahimov, chairman of the department for religious issues, who said that, instead of registering themselves as a religious organisation, the Jehovah's Witnesses were 'conducting religious propaganda, and bribing people'. (SWB)

On 13 January, the Supreme Court confirmed the earlier verdict of Baku City Court that the opposition newspapers *Azadliq, Yeni Musavat, Mukhalifat* and *Hurriyet* were guilty of libelling the family of President Heidar Aliyev (*Index* 1/1999). The newspapers had carried an official speech by rival presidential candidate Ashraf Mehdiyev alleging that Aliyev had Kurdish ancestry and was instrumental in founding Turkey's Kurdish Workers Party (PKK). (Human Rights Centre of Azerbaijan)

Seven supporters of defeated presidential candidate Etibar Mamedov were sentenced to terms of two to three years' hard labour on 9 February after their conviction for hooliganism, resisting arrest, and insulting the honour and dignity of President Heidar Aliyev. The men had participated in an unsanctioned demonstration in Baku on 8 November. (*Turan*, Azerbaijan National Democracy Foundation)

Recent publication: *Monitoring the Media Coverage of the October 1998 Presidential Elections in Azerbaijan – Final Report* (European Institute for the Media, January 1998, 56pp)

BANGLADESH

On 18 January leading poet **Shamur Rahman** avoided an assassination attempt by three members of a new Islamic fundamentalist group, *Harkat-ul-Jihad*. The organisation has allegedly earmarked writer, critic and professor **Kabir Chowdhury**, feminist writer **Taslima Nasrin** and Islamic intellectual **Mawlana Abdul Awal** for assassination because they are 'anti-Islamic'. (Media Watch, International Alliance Against Fundamentalism)

On 24 January feminist writer **Taslima Nasrin** (*Index* 10/1993, 3/1994, 4/1994, 5/1994, 6/1994, 1/1995, 2/1995, 6/1996, 2/1997, 6/1998, 1/1999) left for Sweden after receiving telephone death threats. (Reuters, International Alliance Against Fundamentalism)

Monir Hossain, a reporter with the daily *Dainik Sathkirar Chitra*, was arrested by police on 2 February after his newspaper reported on illegal trade by gangs across the India-Bangladesh border. (RSF)

During a three-day national strike from 9 to 11 February, two newspaper offices were attacked, four vehicles that had been carrying journalists were burnt and four photographers were assaulted. In the worst incident, photographer **Masud Parvez Anis** was shot in the back after trying to take a picture of strikers setting fire to a rickshaw in Dhaka. (Media Watch)

BELARUS

On 22 December the Supreme Economic Court ruled in favour

INDEX INDEX

of the independent weekly *Nasha Niva* which had sued the State Committee on the Press after being charged with using a 'non-Soviet' Belarusian orthography (*Index* 5/1998). After four months of proceedings the court ruled that the use of the traditional spellings, banned since 1933, did not constitute a 'deviation' from accepted norms of the language. The Court also decided to recover 2.5 million rubles in court fees from the State Commission on the Press. (A19)

BENIN

On 15 December **Edouard Loko** and **Septime Tolli**, respectively chief editor and journalist with the independent daily *Le Progrès*, were sentenced to six-month prison terms for slander. The sentence follows a complaint by Abayoi Ganioupar, former director of the Akpakpa college, who was accused in a 31 August article of having mismanaged a fund for summer placement courses. (RSF)

BOTSWANA

Reporter **Andreas Frai** and camerman **Vincent Spiegel** from the Namibia Broadcasting Corporation were arrested in Gaborone on 19 January and charged with 'harassing' dissident Namibians being held at a house pending their trial on charges of illegal entry and carrying weapons. The journalists were released 12 hours later after police had confiscated their video tapes. (MISA)

BULGARIA

On 14 January the public prosecutor opened an investigation into Radio Free Europe journalist **Tatiana Vaksberg**, who is accused of 'attacking honour and dignity' and 'insulting the authority of the state'. Last October Vaksberg made a critical commentary against public prosecutor Ivan Tatcharev, suggesting he was responsible for the impunity of many criminals in the country and might be prosecuted himself for failing to perform his duties. If found guilty she faces up to two years in prison. (RSF)

BURKINA FASO

Norbert Zongo, president of the Private Press Editors' Company and chief editor of the weekly *L'Indépendant*, was found dead in his vehicle on 13 December on the track from Ougadougou to Sapouy. Zongo, whose pen name was Henri Segbo, was a highly respected journalist. (RSF)

CAMBODIA

The government has chosen to allow senior former Khmer Rouge leaders Khieu Samphan and Nuon Chea to escape justice despite the fact the two men are believed to be the key surviving architects in the deaths of over one million Cambodians during the Khmer regime. (AI)

Recent Publication: *Safeguarding Peace: Cambodia's Constitutional Challenge* (Accord, International Review of Peace Initiatives, 1998, pp108)

CAMEROON

On 14 December 1998, **Paul Lois Nyemb Ntoogue**, alias 'Nyemb Popoli', founder of the newspaper *Le Messager-Popoli*, fled to South Africa following a series of threats. He was told by telephone to choose between abandoning his career as a journalist and death by machete. *Le Messager-Popoli* and the main edition of *Le Messager*, have been repeatedly banned and the group's main director, **Pius Njawe**, only received a pardon on 12 October 1998 after spending ten months in prison for 'spreading false information' (*Index* 3/1998, 4/1998, 5/1998, 6/1998). (RSF)

Concern is growing following reports that the health of jailed journalist **Michel Michaut Moussala** is seriously deteriorating (*Index* 2/1998, 6/1998). Moussala has been held in the Central Prison in Douala since September 1998, and is reported to have acute asthma. (AI)

CANADA

Six Health Canada scientists have been ordered not to speak publicly about a bovine growth hormone manufactured by Monsanto, according to an internal document. On 26 October the health department released a statement confirming the document had been prepared by an official, but added that it does 'not reflect the position or policy of the department'. The genetically engineered product was approved by the US in 1993 but is still prohibited in Europe and Canada. (*Globe and Mail*)

On 16 January a British Columbia Supreme Court judge ruled that citizens have a constitutional right to possess child pornography if it is for private use and not distribution. (*Guardian*)

On 5 February, a weekly newspaper in British Columbia, *North Shore News*, was ordered to pay C$1,300 to Harry Abrams for an anti-Semitic editorial written by Doug Collins. Managing editor Tim Renshaw said that the newspaper would challenge the ruling. (The Freedom Forum)

CHAD

On 29 December **Koumbo Singa Gali** and **Polycarpe Togamissi**, respectively chief editor and journalist with the private bi-monthly *L'Observateur*, were each sentenced to a one-year prison term and a fine of CFR500,000 (approx. US$890) following their unsuccessful appeal against their conviction for 'slander' last July (*Index* 4/1998) (RSF)

CHINA

The authorities jammed the Voice of Tibet on 17 December. The Oslo-based radio station broadcasts a 30-minute programme to India, Nepal and Norway. (RSF).

The dissident **Liu Nianchun** was released from labour camp on medical parole and forcibly exiled to the US on 20 December. In a press conference following his exile he said: 'My release into exile for medical treatment cannot be seen as an improvement of China's human rights situation.' (Human Rights in China)

Two Guangdong magazines, *New Weekly* and *Shenzen Pictorial Journal*, were banned by the propaganda department for mentioning the Tiananmen Square incident. *New Weekly* was suspended for four weeks after a December issue mentioned that '32 Beijing hospitals had provided 9,158 medical treatments for the students', a fact omitted from official reports. The *Shenzen Pictorial Journal* has been banned indefinitely. A third Guangzhou-based newspaper, *Cultural Times*, was banned at the end of December for 'circulating outside the province' and, therefore, against the terms of its licence. However the paper's liberal editorial policy seems to be the real motive for its closure. Another newspaper, the *Guangzhou-Hong Kong Daily News*, was ordered to dismiss its management staff by the local Communist Party branch because of 'violations of reporting rules and spreading of liberal bourgeois thought'. (RSF)

Wang Youcai and **Xu Wenli**, founders of the illegal China Democracy Party (CDP), were sentenced to 11 and 13 years' respectively in one-day trials closed to the public on 21 and 22 December in Beijing. Both men were tried on subversion charges. They were forced to present their own defence after their lawyers faced such police harassment that they were unable to represent them. Another CDP organiser, **Qin Youngmin**, was sentenced to 12 years' imprisonment in a

Wuhan court and **Xu Wanping** was sentenced to three years of 're-education through labour' for his involvement in the CDP. (Human Rights in China)

Zhang Lin and **Wei Quanbao**, dissidents who had returned from exile in the US, were sentenced to three years of 'education through labour' on December 27 for having evaded border police and for 'hiring prostitutes'. (*Far East Economic Review*)

Zhang Shanguang was sentenced to 10 years' imprisonment by a court in Hunan province on December 27 for speaking to the US radio station, Radio Free Asia, about rural unrest. Ziang, who spent seven years in prison for his role in the Tiananmen Square demonstrations, was accused of 'illegally providing intelligence to overseas enemy organisations and people'. (*The Times*)

At least 18 people were sentenced to up to 13 years in prison for 'printing or selling illegal publications' on 29 and 30 December. **Wang Suozho** was jailed for publishing more than 15,000 'politically illegal' items between October 1997 and April 1998. A total of 2,800 people have been detained and 190 sentenced during a campaign against illegal books and magazines. (Agence France Presse, Associated Press)

Lin Hai was found guilty of 'incitement to subvert the state' and sentenced to two years in prison on 20 January for providing some 30,000 Chinese e-mail addresses to a US-based on-line magazine, *VIP Reference*

News, run by dissidents in Washington (*Index* 6/1998). Lin Hai's case follows a series of recent attempts by the authorities to step up monitoring of e-mail and internet communications. In the latest tightening of control, police have ordered a special task force to monitor bulletin board services 24 hours a day. When 'counter-revolutionary' notices are found, the police will notify the bulletin board service and seek the name of the sender. (HRW, Associated Press)

Recent publication: Catriona Bass: *Education in Tibet, Policy and Practice since 1950* (Tibet Information Network and Zed Books, 1998)

CHILE

On 18 January the journalist **Paula Afani** was detained and interrogated by the police in an attempt to get her to reveal the sources for a story that appeared in *La Tercera* and *La Hora* newspapers in June 1998. The story concerned the links between the shipping magnate Manuel Losada and a drug-trafficking network known as Ocean Operation. Police also raided Afani's home and the offices of the Consorcio Periodistico de Chile, where the newspapers are based. Six months ago, the State Defence Council proposed restrictive measures on investigations into the Ocean Operation which were rejected by the Valparaiso Court of Appeals. (WAN)

On 27 January lawyers defending former Chilean dictator Augusto Pinochet in the extradition hearing at Britain's House of Lords argued that torture could not be considered a 'crime against humanity' if committed against 'terrorists'. (Equipo Nizkor)

COLOMBIA

On 20 January **Alfredo Molano**, a columnist for the daily *el Espectador*, fled the country after repeated threats against his life. (Comite para la Protección de Periodistas de Colombia)

CONGO-BRAZZAVILLE

The accreditation of **Bienvenu Boudimbou**, a local correspondent with the pan-African radio station Africa No 1, was revoked and its broadcasts suspended on 6 February. Africa No 1 was accused of supporting the opposition by serving as 'a forum for those who carried out the genocide and have found refuge abroad'. (RSF)

CROATIA

On 21 December Zagreb Municipal Court Judge Marin Mrcela once again acquitted *Feral Tribune* editors **Victor Ivancic** and **Marinko Culic** of charges they had insulted President Franjo Tudjman in an April 1996 article and photomontage. The trial had been continually postponed since the appeal court overturned the journalists' previous acquittal in May 1997. Despite this positive outcome the paper still faces over 70 criminal and civil libel suits filed chiefly by public officials and individuals close to the ruling party. (CPJ)

On 20 January *Feral Tribune* announced it was under severe financial pressure because of the withholding of a large sum of money by state-controlled monopoly distributor Tisak. The sum, relating to copies sold in November and December, allegedly amounts to US$207,000 and has created problems in paying staff and its printing house, hence affecting the production of the magazine. The weekly *Nacional* is also owed money by Tisak. (A19, WAN)

CUBA

Milagros Cruz Cano was detained by the police and put into a psychiatric ward on 4 December. Cruz, a member of the banned opposition Democratic Party, had been previously detained in a mental hospital. She was released when doctors unanimously testified to her sanity. (Derechos)

On 6 January security officers detained the director of Havana Press **Jorge Olivera** and correspondents **Jesús Díaz Loyola**, **Lázaro Rodríguez Torres** and **María del Carmen Carro Gómez**. The authorities aimed to prevent the journalists from covering the court hearing for the dissident **Lázaro Constantin Duran**, sentenced to four years in prison for 'dangerousness'. Olivera and Carro were released within hours but Loyola and Rodríguez were held overnight. A week later, on 13 January, two state police detained the independent Cuba Press agency's correspondent, **Odalys Ivettee Curbelo Sánchez**, for several hours and warned her not to cover street demonstrations. (RSF, CPJ).

On 18 January **Hirán González** from Cuba Press was warned by police not to continue passing news to US-funded Radio Martí. The same day, **Jesús Joel Díaz Hernández**, director of the Cooperativa Avileña de Periodistas Independientes (CAPI), was arrested by officers of the Revolutionary National Police. He was sentenced next day to four years in prison for being 'dangerous' and 'breaking socialist norms'. Diaz, who has received six previous warnings, appealed but, on 27 January, a provincial court confirmed the sentence. He was denied legal representation. (RSF, CPJ). **Nancy Sotolongo**, a worker for the Union de Periodistas y Escritores Cubanos Independientes (UPECI), was arrested on 22 January. Four days later, the director of UPECI, **María de los Angeles González**, was also arrested by police who took a tape recorder, cassettes and various documents with them. González was attempting to cover a demonstration to commemorate the anniversary of the visit of Pope John Paul II. A week earlier, she was detained for two nights and prevented from covering a march honouring the birth of Martin Luther King. (RSF, CPJ).

Photographer **Santiago Martínez Trujillo** of UPECI and **Angel Pablo Polanco** of the Cooperativa de Periodistas Independientes (CPI) were arrested on 25 January while preparing to cover a demonstration organised by an illegal human rights organisation. (RSF, CPJ) On 27 January **Pedro Arguelles Morán** of Cuba Press was arrested on the eve of a demonstration in support of human rights. Last year, several journalists were detained for 'insulting' President Fidel Castro, among them **Manuel Antonio González**, correspondent for Cuba Press, who has been in custody since 1 October (*Index* 6/1998) On 28 January Dutch journalist **Edwin Kopman** of Radio Netherlands was expelled for 'giving funds to a counter-revolutionary group'. (RSF, CPJ).

On 2 February Cuba Press journalist **Margarita Yero** received notice from the Housing Office to leave her residence. The measure is thought to be motivated by Yero's professional activities. (RSF)

On 8 December it was reported that **Mbakulu Pambu Diambu**, a journalist with private Radio-Télé Matadi and local president of the Congolese Press Union, had been arrested for having hosted a television show in which he 'welcomed' rebels opposed to President Laurent Kabila as his guests. (RSF)

On 22 December President Kabila is said to have ordered the release of two TV journalists, **Yvette Idi Lupantsha** and **Risasi Risonga**, detained on 19 December 'for being traitors' and for having 'spied for the US'. The two allegedly gave a video cassette of a press conference addressed by President Kabila to US ambassador William Swing. (CPJ, RSF)

Kabeya Pindi Pasi, chief editor of the weekly *Numerica*, was arrested on 23 December and taken to the public prosecutor's office, where he was placed in the 'criminal record' cell for denouncing the poor management of a journalists' organisation and for calling for an accounting of a US$1 million donation by President Kabila to the Congolese press (RSF).

The editor-in-chief of *La Libre Afrique*, **Freddy Loseke Lisumbu**, was arrested on 26 December and given 150 lashes by agents of the presidential security service. He was first questioned concerning his sources for two articles that touched on President Kabila. He was released. (RSF)

Robert Ndaye Tsisense, director of a private TV station, was arrested on 26 December and criticised for not having aired programmes favourable to the president. On 27 December **Mwin Murub Fel**, a journalist with another private TV station was arrested for not having censored a programme which featured an interview with a former political leader who had been recently released from prison. (RSF)

A journalist with twice-weekly *Vision*, **Thierry Kyalumba**, was arrested in Kinshasa and accused of 'disclosing military secrets in war time'. Under the pen name Elvis Bumba,

Kyalumba had published an article suggesting that Uganda had purchased a number of missiles intended for rebel groups active in the Kasai province. (RSF)

Radio Télévision Message de Vie (RTMV) had its studios destroyed by fire on 13 January. The studio owner, **Kurtino Fernado**, a Pentecostal pastor of Angolan nationality, said it was 'highly unlikely' that the fire was accidental. (RSF)

Five journalists from *Potentiel* newspaper were detained on 3 February for publishing articles critical of a new law regulating political parties. The five are **Moise Musangana, Veron-Clement Kongo, Godefroid Ngamisata, Theodore Ngangu** and **Emanuel Katshunga**. (RSF)

EGYPT

On 29 November Tareq Al Awadi, a lawyer, filed suit against President Hosni Mubarak, Prime Minister Kamal Ganzouri and Interior Minister Habi Al Adli demanding the expulsion of Saudi Prince Turki Bin Abdel Aziz for mistreating his Egyptian staff. The prince defended himself by with paid-for spreads in *Al-Arabi* and *Al Shaab* showing servants laughing and testifying to the prince's generosity. Two newpapers, *Al Akhbar* and *Al Wafd*, which carried the original story, have been barred from circulation inside Saudi Arabia for 'publishing incorrect news' and 'defaming the royal family'. (*Cairo Times*)

On 21 December the Higher

Administrative Court accepted a challenge from the Egyptian Organisation for Human Rights against a ministry of social affairs decision denying the organisation legal status under the 1964 association law (*Index*1/99). (Egyptian Organisation for Human Rights)

Abd al Munim Gamal al Din Abd al Munim, an independent journalist working with bi-weekly *Al-Shahab*, who was arrested in February 1993 and detained despite his acquittal in October 1993, has been put on trial along with alleged members of the outlawed *Jihad* movement in Hekstep, North Cairo (*Index* 4/1993, 4/1998). (RSF)

On 8 January **Abbas al-Terabily** and **Mohammed Abdel Alim**, two journalists working for the liberal daily *Al Wafd,* were questioned on suspicion of 'publication of propaganda harming the public interests', after reporting a labour action by central bank workers. (RSF)

ERITREA

Ruth Simon (*Index* 4 /1998, 1/1999) was released from prison on 28 December. The AFP journalist was arrested on 25 April 1997 after publishing reports that quoted President Isayas Aferworki and confirmed the presence of Eritrean soldiers fighting alongside Sudanese rebels. (IFJ)

Recent publications: Roy Rateman, 1998 *Eritrea: Even the Stones Are Burning*, (Red Sea Publications (revised edition),

239pp, Price US$12.95)

ETHIOPIA

Jailed surgeon **Professor Asrat Woldeyes** (*Index* 1/1999) was released from prison on 27 December. He was reported to have been in a very critical condition. (AAASHRAN, AI, Ethiopian Democratic Action League, *Guardian*)

Recent publications: *Fire from the Ashes: Chronicle of the Revolution in Tigray, Ethiopia,* : Jenny Hammond, 1998.

EUROPEAN UNION

The corruption scandal involving EU commissioners continued in December and January with further evidence of impropriety. Agenor SA, the Belgian company which runs the commission's £400m Leonardo project supervising training for the unemployed, is alleged to have evaded tax and dispensed appointments to family members. The allegations, based upon a leaked internal report by EU auditor **Paul van Buitenen**, also tarnished the reputation of Commissioner Edith Cresson, a former French prime minister now responsible for education and training. Van Buitenen, frustrated by the EU's apparent indifference to systemic fraud, wrote directly to MEPs in early January to state publicly that the EC had obstructed investigations into the various allegations (*Index* 5/1998). The EU responded to van Buitenen's allegations by suspending him from duty for 'imparting information to unauthorised and non-competent persons'. The allegations sparked a censure vote in the European Parliament which threatened to remove some, or all, of the 20 European Commissioners. The majority Socialist group in the parliament, however, voted against censure, as long as the EU agreed to closer supervision by MEPs. (*Guardian, Daily Telegraph, The Times*)

FIJI ISLANDS

Fiji Times is facing the threat of action by the House of Representatives' Privileges Committee over an editorial published on 1 December. The editorial questioned the cost of meetings of new backbench parliamentary committees and the lack of provision for these in the budget. Labour Party leader Mahendra Chaudry claims that the *Fiji Times* 'was maliciously critical of parliamentarians without verifying the facts'. (Pacific Islands News Association)

On 9 February, three months before the first general elections, the government became the biggest shareholder in the *Daily Post* newspaper, buying US505,000 worth of shares (44 per cent of the stock) from the Fiji Development Bank. (Pacific Islands News Association)

GABON

Broadcasts by private radio station *Radio Soleil* were jammed beginning 7 December. The same day a statement by the National Communication Council (CNC) criticised the station for a programme in which it allowed listeners to phone in and denounce any

fraudulent activities which they witnessed during the casting of ballots during the presidential election of 6 December. (RSF)

GEORGIA

As 1998 drew to a close, Tanamgzavri TV correspondent **Nato Megutnishvili** was fired for her coverage of a political kidnapping in Telavi for the national news magazine programme *Kvira*. The story arose after the ruling Citizens Union of Georgia (CUG) lost its majority on Telavi's city council after the 15 November election. To better manipulate the voting arithmetic, the CUG kidnapped an opposition councillor in advance of the council's first meeting. (Internews)

GERMANY

In December journalists from the Berlin newspaper *Tageszeitung* appealed to the Supreme Court to curb the surveillance powers of the BND, the foreign intelligence service. Under 1994 legislation, the BND is empowered to run a computer-monitored keyword search on all international phone, fax and telephone traffic. *Tageszeitung* argued that BND should not be able to monitor calls between its editors and its Rome-based correspondent who covers Mafia investigations. The BND argues that the powers are essential to combat the international drugs trade and terrorism. *Tageszeitung* argued that besides the BND's activities being a contravention of press freedom, the intelligence service was acting unconstitutionally 'as an extended arm of the police'.

(*Guardian*)

On 15 January it was reported that media giant Bertelsmann has launched an internal inquiry into its own activities during the Nazi era, following allegations that the company had published propaganda for the Hitler regime. American-Israeli historian Saul Friedlander has been appointed to lead the independent inquiry. (*International Herald Tribune, Guardian*)

GREECE

On 23 December in Skopje, Macedonia, Foreign Affairs Minister Theodoros Pangalos called all persons in the Greek region of western Macedonia 'pervert intellectuals and pervert journalists'. Arguing that the minority was artificial, he referred to its representative political party as 'a coalition of Slavo-Macedonians, Stalinists and homosexuals'. On 19 January Pangalos accused Greek journalists of being the worst enemies of the government, after one posed what he perceived to be an embarrassing question on Greek-Bulgarian relations. (Greek Helsinki Monitor)

On 21 January the Appeals Court of the Aegean cleared **Yannis Tzoumas**, journalist and publisher of the Chios island daily *Alithia*, of defamation charges. Tzoumas was convicted on 3 September and sentenced to four months' imprisonment after 'defaming' a minister, Stavros Soumakis. Although the first trial accepted the article's facts were correct, the court considered the 'harsh style' of the article constituted an act of defamation. The Appeals Court agreed there had been no attempt to defame the minister but only to criticise his behaviour, albeit in a 'harsh style'. (Greek Helsinki Monitor)

GUATEMALA

A 3,500-page truth commission report on the 36-year civil war has been completed. It includes information on some 8,000 massacres, tortures, disappearances and assassinations by both army and the rebels, most committed when violence peaked in the early 1980s. The Historical Clarification Commission will present its report to President Alvaro Arzu, ex-guerrilla leaders and a representative of the UN secretary-general at a ceremony on 25 February. The report has been criticised by human rights advocates because it does not name individuals and its findings cannot be used in prosecutions. (Reuters)

On 17 February Judge Henry Monroy ordered the release for lack of evidence of the ailing priest **Mario Orantes**, the sole suspect in the murder of **Archbishop Juan José Gerardi** last April (*Index* 4/1998). Orantes, who found Gerardi bludgeoned to death in the house where they lived, is is still formally accused though the case has temporarily been closed. Gerardi was killed two days after presenting the Catholic Church's own landmark report on human rights violations which attributed 90 per cent of violations to the armed forces. 'There is a very clear campaign

to discredit the Catholic Church and Monsignor Gerardi's memory,' said a Catholic spokesman. (Reuters)

On 17 January a group of assailants broke into the office of the daily *La Hora* and took away documentation. The newspaper's executive committee planned to meet on 19 January to discuss measures to counteract attempts to limit freedom of expression. (Press Freedom Committee of the Guatemalan Journalists Association)

GUINEA

Mouctar Ba, a correspondent of Agence France-Presse (AFP) and Radio France Internationale (RFI), had his accreditation annulled on 24 December by the National Council on Communications (CNC). In a letter to AFP and RFI management, CNC president Emile Tompapa said the 'tendentious, whimsical and malicious character of the information' reported by the journalist was the reason for his decision. Ba was not given the opportunity to respond directly to the accusations. (RSF)

Don de Dieu Agoussou, a journalist of Béninois nationality at the weekly *L'Oeil*, was expelled on 29 January. He had gone to the Gbessia Conakry airport to cover the arrival of heads of state invited to the swearing-in ceremony of President Lansana Condé. At the airport, he was put on a Ghana Airways flight to Bénin. Agoussou had previously received a warning from the counter-espionage services after

the 29 July publication of an article entitled 'Power – journalist, what future?' (RSF)

INDIA

On 1 January a crowd of 60 to 70 youths set a Pentacostal prayer hall on fire in the Dang tribal area of Gujarat. The burning was one of a series of incidents in which ecclesiasts were attacked and churches burnt after Christmas. (Reuters)

Shivani Bhatnagar, a member of the investigations team at the *Indian Express*, was murdered at her home by unknown assailants on 23 January. Bhatnagar had phoned her husband that day to say that two men had delivered an invitation to a wedding. Her killers may have been trying to recover certain documents. (CPJ, RSF)

Salman Rushdie was granted a visa on 4 February to visit the country of his birth for the first time since rioting by outraged Muslims led to the banning of his novel, *The Satanic Verses*, a decade ago. Muslim groups accused the government of 'playing with their emotions'. (*Guardian, Asian Age*)

On 6 February the Bangiya Christian Pariseba, a united forum of Catholics and Protestants, revealed that the head of the Calcutta Bible Society was told that he would be killed if the Society did not stop publishing the Bible. Similar threats have also been received by Bible societies in Orissa and Tamil Nadu. (*Asian Age*)

On 10 February **Naresh**

• •

BOIPU
Burning the hand that feeds

S^{ir,}

For years, India has maintained its secular credentials and prevented religion from becoming a divisive force. However, the recent spurt of violence and attacks on the minorities, especially Christians, has shaken many in India. Religion is a personal choice, a bond between an individual and the holy spirit. The state needn't interfere in the personal faith of its citizens. Instead of honouring a missionary like Graham Steward Staines, we mercilessly burnt him and his innocent sons. Some sections in India are under the wrong impression that they have eliminated someone who, according to them, was indulging in mass conversion. Conversion is not a one-night process and is never achieved through force. It is a matter of one's faith and decision. And what is wrong if one's finds solace in a particular religion and decides to accept that faith? Where is the spirit of democracy enshrined in the Indian Constitution which entitles freedom of religion? Are we any different from our neighbouring theocratic states? It is a known fact that, if Graham Steward Staines had wanted, he could have led a comfortable life. Still he chose to come to one of the most remote villages of India to serve humanity. By burning him alive, we bit the very hand that fed us. The least one can do is to share the grief of Esther and her mother in this hour of shame. ❏

The above letter, from a correspondent in Greater Kailash II, New Delhi, was published in the letters page of the newspaper Asian Age *on 8 February 1999. On 23 January* **Graham Steward Staines** *and his sons* **Philip** *and* **Timothy** *were burned to death in their vehicle by a mob of 50 to 100 people in the state of Orissa. Cadres of the* Bajrang Dal – *the militant wing of the World Hindu Council – were reportedly responsible.*

• •

Kalita, news editor of the vernacular daily *Agradoot*, was arrested on charges of aiding and abetting separatists in the state of Assam. Kalita's colleagues claim that his arrest is part of 'a conspiracy by the Assam government to gag the voice of the press'. (RSF)

On 14 February the Central Board of Film Certification re-approved the controversial film *Fire* for distribution, saying that no cuts were needed. Last December, Hindu fundamentalists attacked numerous cinemas showing the film because it portrays a lesbian relationship (*Index* 1/1999). (Press Trust of India)

INDONESIA

Jakarta police on 29 December summoned **Abdul Manaf**, managing editor of the new bi-weekly *Warta Republik*, to answer allegations of defamation following a lawsuit lodged by Try Sutrisno, the former vice-president. Police spokesman Lieutenant-Colonel Aritonang alleged the paper had gone too far in abusing press freedom and had not provided objective coverage in its story of illicit and competitive affairs between two cabinet members over a widow. (*Jakarta Post*)

President Habibi on 5 January noted that an important part of the democratising process was freedom of the press. But he expressed concern over what he believed was abuse of press freedom, claiming that 'exaggerated or unbalanced reports have the potential to cause social confusion and unrest.' (ANTARA)

IRAN

It was announced on 5 January that two weeklies, *Shalamcheh* and *Fakour* had been suspended after convictions by the Press Court in Tehran. *Shalamcheh*, a hard-line weekly, was banned after publishing information regarding the relationship between the late Ayatollah Abolqassem al-Khoei and the Shah's secret police. *Fakour*, a moderate publication, had its publishing licence revoked, but no reason has been given. (RSF)

The Intelligence Ministry announced on 6 January that 'rogue elements' within its own ranks had murdered five secular intellectuals last November and December, and that several agents had been arrested (*Index* 1/1999). Many Iranians suspected the killings had been committed by conservatives opposed to liberalization, but few expected such an open declaration of culpability. (*Guardian, Daily Telegraph, International Herald Tribune*)

On 2 February a court banned the liberal cultural journal *Adineh*, after finding the bi-weekly's editor, **Gholam Hussein Zekeri**, 'guilty of insult and dissemination of lies and corrupt articles'. Zekeri was ordered to pay US$1,035. (IPI)

Zan ('Woman'), Iran's first publication aimed at a female audience, was banned for two weeks on 24 January following charges by the head of police security, Mohammad Naki. An article in the daily had accused Naki of involvement in an attack on Vice-President Abdollah Nuri and Minister of Culture Ata'ollah Mohejerani in front of Tehran University in September. On 7 February the state news agency IRNA reported that *Zan* had been allowed to resume publication. (IPI)

IRAQ

It was reported on 4 February that some governmental offices will soon have access to the internet, according to Hilal al-Bayati, director of Iraq's National Computer Center. Al-Bayati said in the *al-Zawra* weekly that access would be limited to ensure that Iraqi users are not affected 'by negative Western thoughts,' and that the net would be used to transmit 'genuine' Iraqi culture. (Iraq Foundation)

IRELAND

On 13 January it was reported that Sarah Flannery, a schoolgirl from Blarney, had devised a encryption method for sending e-mail that is ten times faster than the standard code devised by three students at the Massachusetts Institute of Technology. Flannery – who has been bombarded with job offers – confounded judges at the Irish Young Scientists and Technology Exhibition when she said she had no intention of patenting her discovery since she did not want people to have to pay for it. (Associated Press, *The Times*)

JORDAN

On 4 February **Fahd Rimawi**, editor of *Al-Majd*, was served a 15-day detention order for violating the national press code

• •

MOHAMMAD POUYANDEH, ALI ASHRAF DARVISHIAN, MAHMOUD DOLATABADI, KAZEM KARDAVANI, MANSOUR KOUSHAN, HOUSHANG GOLSHIRI, MOHAMMAD MOKHTARI

Dangerous words

1. Freedom of opinion and expression in every sphere of individual and social life is the right of everyone without limits or exceptions. The right is not the monopoly of any person, group or institution, and no one can be deprived of it.

2. The Writers' Association of Iran is opposed to any kind of censorship of opinion or expression, and calls for the removal of all procedures which, officially or unofficially, prevent the publication or dissemination of works and viewpoints.

3. The Association considers the growth and developments of the country's different languages to be one of the pillars of the enhancement of culture and of understanding and fellow-feeling between all Iranians, and it is opposed to any kind of discrimination or elimination regarding the publication, dissemination and distribution of works in all languages.

4. The Association is opposed to monotonality in all visual, audio and computer media, and calls for the creation of multi-tonal media in every cultural sphere.

5. It is the natural, human and civil right of writers to have their works arrive in the hands of their audience without any impediment. It goes without saying that everyone has the right to criticise freely.

6. Words must be answered with words; however, when a dispute arises about a work, it is the responsibility of the Writers' Association of Iran to offer its professional opinion in establishing the truth of the claim.

7. The Association defends the material and moral rights, social honour and physical, professional and occupational security of Iranian writers.

8. The Writers' Association of Iran is independent and not affiliated in any governmental or non-governmental institution (group, party, club, organisation etc.)

9. Co-operation between the members of the Association must – while maintaining their individual independence – be based on the aims set out in this charter.

10. The Writers' Association of Iran will cooperate with people or organisations in connection with the rights, aims and ideals set out in this charter, where this co-operation does not contravene the principles and positions of the Association. ❏

This draft charter was published last August in Adineh. *Two of its signatories,* **Mohammad Pouyandeh** *and* **Mohammad Mokhtari**, *were murdered by 'rogue elements' inside the Intelligence Ministry in late 1998.*

• •

by giving a full account of the late King Hussein's deposing of Hassan as crown prince. Censors also barred the sale of *The Times*, *Sunday Times* and *Sunday Telegraph* because of their coverage of palace intrigues and the King's health. As part of the same effort to restrict information, the board chairman of the weekly *Al-Arab al-Yawm* sacked two senior editors after they published unofficial reports on the changes in the succession. **Taher al-Adwwan** and **Saleh al-Kallab** said they had been given no reason for their dismissal. *(The Times)*

KAZAKHSTAN

In the run-up to the 10 January presidential election, a court in Karaganda suspended publication of the newspaper *Soroka* until 8 January on the pretext that it had failed to indicate the place of printing on its masthead. Tax police officers froze the bank accounts of an Astana newspaper, *Center*, preventing it from publishing from October 1998 until 12 January 1999. More subtle pressures on other newspapers meant that incumbent President Nursultan Nazarbayev dominated pre-election coverage in all but the independent newspapers *451 Gradusa po Farengeitu (Fahrenheit 451)*, *XXI Vek (21st Century)* and the now-closed *Dat (Index 1/1999)*. On national television, Nazarbayev received 76 per cent of all air time devoted to electoral candidates. (Glasnost Defence Foundation)

KENYA

The *Daily Nation*, Kenya's largest selling daily, was on 21 December barred from covering proceedings at the Akiwumi Commission investigating tribal clashes that rocked the country between 1992 and 1997. The paper was accused of 'contempt of commission' for publishing a report without 'consulting the commission'. (Ndima)

The High Court on 22 December restrained the publisher of *Finance* magazine, **Njehu Gatabaki**, from publishing articles linking cabinet minister Nicholas Biwott to the murder of former foreign affairs minister Robert Ouko, who was killed in February 1990 (*Index 1/1997, 2/1998*). (Media Institute, Ndima)

An *East African Standard* correspondent, **Mohammed Sheikh Muthay**, was held on 4 February and questioned over a story he wrote on an ethnic massacre in Danyere division of Garissa district. (*Daily Nation*)

MPs **David Mwenje, James Orengo** and **Njehu Gatabaki** (*Index 2/1998*) were arrested on 2 February and charged with inciting university students to riot. The three were engaged in a campaign to save Karura forest from destruction by developers who want to build luxury apartments. (*Guardian*, Media Institute, *Daily Nation*)

Eastern provincial commissioner, Nicholas Mberia, on 11 February ejected journalists from a meeting called to discuss insecurity in Isiolo,

Marsabit and Moyale districts. (*East African Standard*)

KUWAIT

During the mid-December military strike on Iraq, a journalist who reported the whereabouts of the RAF was forced to broadcast a retraction saying that British warplanes were not using Kuwait as a base for their attacks. (*The Times*)

On 26 December **Fouad al-Hashem** was sentenced to three months in prison for an article he wrote in June 1997 for the daily *Al-Watan*. His jocular article concerned controversial travel expenses paid by an oil company to prosecutors who were investigating alleged embezzlement by their own officials. The court deemed the article 'insulting to public prosecutors'. (RSF)

KYRGYZSTAN

The Commission on Ethics in the Media, created by the Justice Ministry on 6 October 1998, was abolished on 25 January. At the commission's first meetings in October, it had called for the closure of three independent newspapers, *Paishamba*, *Limon* and *Kaptama-Digest*, accusing them of pornography (*Index 1/1999*). The criminal cases were dropped after their owners reached amicable agreements with the Justice Ministry. (Kyrgyz News)

LESOTHO

On 28 January, **Candi Ramainoane**, editor of *MoAfrika* newspaper (*Index 1/1999*), was called to appear before Advocate Justice Cullinan on charges of contempt of court regarding an article published in the 22 January issue of the newspaper. Justice Cullinan is presiding over the court martial at which 49 soldiers are facing possible death sentences on treason charges. On 19 January he was denied access to the court martial because, according to one military policeman, 'orders are that you are not to be allowed in'. (MISA)

On 26 November the South African National Defence Force (SANDF) again targeted **Naleli Ntlamahad**, a freelance journalist and columnist with the *Public Eye* newspaper (*Index* 1/1999). Soldiers came to Ntlama's house while he was away and left a message with neighbours that 'they will be back for him tonight'. When the neighbours asked what they wanted, the soldiers told them that Ntlama had opened a case against them saying that they had destroyed his property and they wanted evidence of the damage. (MISA)

LIBERIA

On 23 November, a group of former combatants in the on-going conflict stormed the Sabannoh Printing Press, attacked journalists and employees, destroyed copies of the independent *Inquirer* and the *News* newspapers, and vandalised printing machinery. The attack was in response to a 21 November front-page story in the *Heritage* newspaper, titled 'Ex-Fighters Plan Mass Demonstration', which claimed that former combatants planned to demand benefits from the government. The Sabannoh Printing Press is also the printer for *Heritage*. **J. Kpanquor Jallah Jr.**, the *Heritage* reporter who wrote the story, was briefly detained but was released after colleagues demanded that police produce a warrant for his arrest. **Nagbe**, a journalist with the *News*, received a deep laceration on his back during the attack. He was reportedly pointed out as a journalist by a security guard assigned to protect the press. Neither government security guards, posted at Sabannoh since the commencement of the 18 September fighting in Monrovia, nor the armed police officers who arrived on the scene, intervened to stop the vandalism or assaults. (CPJ)

MACEDONIA

On 29 January **Gorica Popova** was demoted from her editorial position to that of 'junior associate' by the new general director of state-owned Radio and Television, Ljupcho Jakimovski, for her commentary on a memorial service in Novo Selo in honour of the controversial inter-war historical figure **Todor Aleksandrov**. (Greek Helsinki Monitor)

MALAYSIA

The prosecution in the trial of **Anwar Ibrahim** has proposed to amend the charges against the former deputy prime minister from alleged acts of sexual misconduct to mere 'allegations'. The move reduces the burden of proof needed to secure a conviction as the prosecution no longer has to prove that Ibrahim committed adultery or sodomy, only that he used his influence to quash police investigations. (Associated Press, *International Herald Tribune*, *Far Eastern Economic Review*)

MEXICO

After an extensive search carried out by the military, **Philip True**, correspondent for the US-based *San Antonio Express-News*, was discovered dead on 15 December at the bottom of a ravine. Forensic evidence made public by the medical examiner in Jalisco showed that True had been strangled and sexually assaulted, as well as receiving head injuries not caused by a fall. True was last seen alive in the village of Chalmotottia on 4 December after he had left his Mexico City home for a trip through Sierra Madre Occidental in Nayarit and Jalisco states where he had planned to work on a project on the local Huichol Indians. (RSF)

MONGOLIA

Mongolia enacted a new media law on 1 January that forbids state ownership of news media and requires existing state-owned newspapers to be privatised. The effects have mainly been seen on mastheads: *Government News* has become *Century News* and *People's Right* has become *National Right*. (Associated Press)

MOZAMBIQUE

The Maputo daily *Noticias* of 26 January reported that journalist **Fernando Quinova**, correspondent for the state-owned Mass Communications Institute in the Cabo Delgado district of Chiure, had been detained for 23 days because he denounced police brutality. Quinova wrote a story about an alleged thief, Cabral Manica, who died through torture. After publishing the story, which was broadcast on Radio Mozambique in mid-December, police arrested Quinova for 'sullying' the reputation of the police. No charges were laid against the reporter, who was kept in the police cells for 23 days. Quinova said that police demanded 100,000 meticais (US$8) for the privilege of 'seeing the sun' during his period of detention. It was on one of these occasions that he managed to escape. (MISA)

NAMIBIA

Another TV crew from the South African Broadcasting Corporation (SABC) was briefly detained in the Caprivi Strip on 24 November while reporting on tension in that area, according to the Namibian newspaper (Index 1/1999). It was the second SABC crew to be detained in less than a week. The two crew members, journalist **Jessica Pitchford** and camera operator **Dudley Saunders**, were held by security forces in Linyata after they apparently strayed into a restricted area. The two were part of a group of foreign and local journalists invited to the Caprivi region by Namibia's Information and Broadcasting Ministry in the wake of increased military activity in the area following reports of an alleged secessionist plot. (MISA)

Prime Minister Hage Geingob has admitted that the Ministry of Defence is deliberately withholding information about its involvement in war in the Democratic Republic of Congo. Geingob confirmed in a letter to the independent Namibian that Minister of Defence Erikki Nghimtina 'had instructed his staff not to release any information to the media generally, because of a number of reasons.... Rest assured, information is not being held back only from the Namibian, but from all newspapers.' (MISA)

In February, the Namibian and the National Broadcasting Corporation (NBC) reached an out-of-court settlement with five police and military officers, who were poised to sue the two organisations for defamation. The matter was due to come before court on 8 February. (MISA)

NEPAL

On 25 November **Yadu Lamichhane**, editor of the political monthly Himalayan Journal, was arrested and jailed at Bhadragol prison in Kathmandu. Last August Lamichhane was arrested for 'being Maoist', but he was released when the Supreme Court failed to find him guilty of any offence. On 15 December **Rishiraj Baral**, editor-in-chief of the weekly Yojana, was also arrested for 'being Maoist'. A month earlier, Baral had been detained after covering a demonstration against the killing of civilians by the army, and jailed between 14 and 23 November for 'diffusing

propaganda that creates chaos in society'. (RSF)

On 5 January the police arrested four journalists in Kathmandu for 'having links with Maoists', after an allegedly illegal raid on the office of the weekly Janadesh. The journalists have been identified as **Rebati Sapkota**, editor of the weekly Mahima, **Shakti Lamsal**, consulting editor of the weeklies Janadesh and Yojana, **Dhana Bahadur Magar**, office manager of the weeklies Janadesh and Yojana,and **Ashok Subedi**, a freelance journalist working for Himalayan Times. In its 5 January issue, Janadesh published the pictures of two policemen reportedly killed by rebels of the Maoist Communist Party of Nepal. The editors of Janadesh are currently in hiding. (RSF)

NETHERLANDS

At a parliamentary inquiry on 3 February the government admitted that it had known that an Israeli plane which crashed into a block of flats in Amsterdam in 1992 had been carrying ammunition, explosives and flammable and toxic gases. The inquiry was established after persistent complaints of illness from surviving residents. The transport minister at the time, Hanja Maij, said that she had never been told about the cargo and that she felt 'deceived and disillusioned' by the disclosure. (Guardian)

NIGERIA

Lucky Odijie, senior photojournalist with the Daily Times, was severely beaten on 31 December by security officers at

Oshodi, Lagos. Odije was accosted by security men in a commercial bus which they had impounded. He protested that he be allowed to disembark from the bus but the men, irritated by his demand, beat him up. 'We have killed you people before so yours will not be the first,' one of the soldiers said before dumping Idijie at the roadside. (Nigeria Media Monitor)

Information Minister John Nwodo has hinted at plans to make libel a criminal offence. Addressing journalists in Calabar, Cross Rivers, in December, Nwodo said: 'I am thinking of criminalising libel because of the fact that people libel their fellows and get away with it.' He cited a recent article which claimed that he patronised a spiritualist named Guru Maharaji Ji so that 'he could be appointed minister'. Nwodo argued that, if falsehoods could be published against him despite his position, the ordinary man had no hope, especially as civil action could be tedious, protracted and expensive. (IPR)

On 27 January Information Minister John Nwodo said in Abuja that the government would amend the Press Council Law to give it more 'teeth'. He said the amendment is necessary in view of the fact that the laws controlling the practice of journalism had become 'licentious'. (Media Monitor)

There is growing concern about jailed journalist **Niran Malaolu** (*Index* 2/1998, 3/1998, 4/1998, 5/1998, 1/1999), who is reportedly being denied urgent medical treatment despite his rapidly deteriorating health. His wife, Bukola, said he has still not been treated for typhoid fever he contracted several months ago and is complaining of pain and headaches and had water and pus constantly gushing out of his eyes. (PEN)

On 8 February police officers stormed the editorial offices of the *News* and the premises of 24 Hours press, arresting general manager **Idowu Obasa**, press manager **Wole Odofin** and **Tajudeen Suleiman**. The journalists were released without charge later in the night. (IPR)

PAKISTAN

In early November **Hashim Paktyanie**, a prominent journalist advocating a parliamentary system of government in Afghanistan, was gunned down as he left his house in Peshawar. On 9 November **Dagarwal Latif** was assassinated in Quetta by gunmen on a motorbike. His killing appears linked to his support for a political solution to the conflict in Afghanistan. Sixteen days later, **General Shirin Agha**, a leading member of *Da Solh Ghorazan* (Peace Movement Party), was shot dead in Peshawar. On 27 November **Ata Mohammed Sarkatib**, known for his oppositon to Taliban policies, was seriously wounded at his home by several armed men. (*Index* 1/1998). (AI)

On 26 November the home of **Indrees Bakhtiar**, a senior staff reporter of the *Herald* monthly and correspondent for the BBC, was raided by police in connection with the recent murder of Hakim Saeed, the ex-governor of Sindh province. Bakhtiar's son Moonis was briefly detained and questioned about the whereabouts of one of the prime suspects in the case. The police later claimed that the raid had been an honest mistake. (Pakistan Press Foundation)

The Karachi home of **Naseer Ahmad Saleemi**, bureau chief of the weekly *Zindagi*, was raided by police on 27 November. Saleemi's brother, Bashir Ahmad Saleemi, was arrested, but then released on the order of Farooq Amin Quereshi, the deputy inspector general of police. Police claim the raid was conducted after a passport, which bore Saleemi's address, was recovered from a terrorist allegedly involved in the 1994 murder of **Salahuddin**, the editor of *Takbeer* newspaper. (Pakistan Press Foundation)

Since August 1998 the Jang Group, the country's largest newspaper company, has been put under extensive pressure by Prime Minister Nawaz Sharif's government to avoid reporting politically sensitive stories. In mid-December, the daily *Jang's* publication of articles about a financial scandal involving the Prime Minister's Ittefaq Group of Companies, which had first appeared in the London *Observer*, led to a raid on it's Rawalpindi bureau by officers of the Federal Investigation Agency. **Mir Shakil-ur-Rahman**, publisher and editor-in-chief, alleged that the government applied intense pressure not to print the article, but he resisted. Subsequently, the central government ratcheted-up tax arrears allegations against the group, despite the fact that the Income Tax Appelate Court had yet to review the merits of the case; the company's bank accounts were temporarily frozen; various government departments made it near impossible for *Jang* to obtain sufficient newsprint; and Senator Saifur Rahman, who heads the government's *Ehtesab* (Accountability) Bureau, repeatedly asked Shakil-ur-Rahman to dismiss several reporters who are on a government 'blacklist'. (Freedom House, RSF, Pakistan Press Foundation, CPJ, *Asian Age*)

Zafarayab Ahmed (*Index* 6/1998) was finally allowed on 15 December to take up his fellowship and teaching duties at Colby College in the US. Despite this development, Ahmed still faces charges of high treason for research he did on child labour. (Canadian Journalists for Free Expression)

On 17 December two armed men barged into the Peshawar home of **Saeed Iqbal Hashmi**, chief reporter of the Urdu-language daily *Mashriq* (*Index* 6/1998). Hashmi was not at home and his would-be assassins were scared off by his relatives. Hashmi later received a telephone death threat from a man with an Afghan accent: 'Whenever we get the chance, we will kill you for your enmity with the Islamic government of the Taliban.' (RSF, CPJ)

On 8 January **Muradam Mai**, a diagnosed paranoid schizophrenic of Soriaki ethnic

origin, was horribly disfigured and burned to death by a gang of men in the village of Chak 100P in Punjab Province. The assailants justified their actions on the grounds that Mai had been found sitting in the village shrine burning pages from its Koran. One participant quipped that 'she burnt the Koran, so we burnt her'. But other sources suggest Mai had been burning paper charms given her by a local holy man in the hope that her mental health would be restored. (*Independent*)

On 13 January the district administration of Makaland in North West Fontier Province (NWFP) released **Syed Rasool Rasa**, the Batkela-based correspondent for the Urdu daily *Khabrain*, after six days of incarceration. Rasa was arrested after the publication of an article reporting the arrest of a member of the NWFP provincial legislature. (RSF)

In another attack against Peshawar-based newspapers and jounalists, three unidentified men ransacked the offices of the English-language *Khyber Mail International* on 30 January. Messenger Mohammed Javed was beaten severely during the incident. (Pakistan Press Foundation)

Maleeha Lodhi, editor of the *News* of Islamabad, informed Interior Minister Chaudary Shujat Hussain in a 31 January letter that she had received death threats over the phone. Lodhi also said that, although she had received similar threats in the past, the latest were more ominous because of the current hostility between the

government and the Jang Group, which publishes the *News*. (Pakistan Press Foundation)

After extensive agitation by journalist's groups and opposition politicians – at home and abroad – against the government's crackdown against the Jang Group of newspapers, the information minister reported on 7 February that 'all issues have been amicably resolved to the satisfaction of both sides'. (Freedom House, RSF, Pakistan Press Foundation, CPJ, *Asian Age*)

On 7 December **Adda Oushpiz**, correspondent for the Israeli daily *Ha'aretz*, was shot in the leg with rubber bullets while covering clashes between Palestinians and Israeli soldiers in the West Bank town of Ramallah. Oushpiz was the eleventh journalist to be shot by Israeli forces in 1998. (RSF)

Seven media stations were closed down on 18 December during the US/UK military strikes on Iraq. In Ramallah, Radio Peace and Love, Watan TV and Nasr TV were ordered to suspend activities, as were Al-Roa' TV, Al-Mahid TV and Bethlehem TV in Bethlehem, and Associated Press in Gaza. Captain Ali Ghuneim informed managers that the order had come from a 'high ranking official' yet the minister responsible, Yasser Abed Rubbo, denied any knowledge of the ban. In the wake of the Wye River Agreement the closures would be in line with President

Arafat's sweeping Anti-Incitement Decree of November 1998, which banned activities that 'provoke the public to the break the covenants agreed upon by the PLO and neighbouring foreign countries.' (RSF, *Guardian*)

PANAMA

On 28 December the police raided the offices of *La Prensa*, leaving a written order for the detention of investigative reporter **Herasto Reyes**. The police had orders to take Reyes to the prosecutor's office accused of defaming President Ernesto Perez Balladares over an August 1998 interview with former president Manuel Noriega. In the interview, Noriega accused Balladares of trying to force him to cover up major financial malfeasance. (CPJ)

PAPUA NEW GUINEA

On 26 January the Media Council of Papua New Guinea expressed alarm over recent funding cuts, which include the closure of the University of New Guinea's 23-year-old journalism course. Council president Luke Sela said: 'We particularly see the closure of the journalism course as having a direct and negative impact upon developing skilled thinkers to record and disseminate accurate and meaningful information for the benefit of our people.' (*National*)

Defenders of press freedom are mounting a campaign to head off a takeover bid of the *Papua New Guinea Post-Courier*, the largest-selling daily newspaper, by associates of Prime Minister Bill Skate. (BBC)

PERU

On 2 December journalist **Cesar Hildebrandt** prematurely terminated his agreement with Canal 13 Global Television complaining that in less than two months his programme was taken off the air on three occasions (*Index* 1/1998, 5/1998, 6/1998, 1/1999). The director and manager of the production company offered assurances that technical reasons were responsible for forcing the programme off the air. (Instituto de Prensa y Sociedad)

A Peruvian Court ordered on 4 December the arrest of the television executive **Baruch Ivcher** for doctoring the station's ownership registry (*Index* 4/1997, 5/1997, 6/1997, 2/1998, 3/1998, 4/1998, 5/1998, 6/1998, 1/1999). The court said Ivcher's wife and daughter Neomy Even and Michal Ivcher were also involved and issued arrests warrants for them as well. (Instituto de Prensa y Sociedad, Freedom Forum)

On 9 December **Johny Eduardo Pezo** was jailed for having read a letter sent by the Tupac Amaru Revolutionary Movement on his radio programme. The 23-year-old journalist was allegedly forced to read the letter by the armed group in his music programme. Pezo was released on 18 January. (Instituto de Prensa y Sociedad)

On 10 December the director of the news programme *Opinión* of Radio Uranio, **Irwin Barrios**, was physically attacked by the mayor of the province who was offended by his on-air criticism. After defending himself, the journalist was arrested and remained in jail for 24 hours for beating the mayor. (Instituto de Prensa y Sociedad)

On 17 December, two months after going into hiding, the journalist **Jose Luis Bardales** gave IPYS an exclusive interview to be released only outside Peru. The former director of the bi-weekly magazine *Quincenario Matutino* and director of the *Matutino* news programme of Radio Panamericana was forced to abandon his home and job after four men got into his car and said that, if he did leave town in 24 hours, they would kill him. (Instituto de Prensa y Sociedad)

On 9 January journalist **Carlos Caldas Pozo** had his programme, *La Alternativa* on Radio Exito FM, shut down. He aired news that accused Italo Valle Pachas, owner of a construction company, of misappropriating his employee's wages. Prior to the event, Caldas was told to refrain himself from criticising the businessman, who tried to interfere by buying radio time to broadcast his own independent newscasts. . (Instituto de Prensa y Sociedad)

ROMANIA

On 4 December the opposition Social Democracy Party filed suit against the government for agreeing to found a multi-ethnic university with courses taught in Hungarian and German, on the grounds that it would contravene the constitution. (SWB)

On 18 January **Ovidiu Scultenicu** and **Dragos Stangu**, journalists with the independent weekly *Monitorul*, were sentenced to suspended one-year prison terms for slandering police colonel Petru Susanu in an article that criticised his methods and questioned the origins of his wealth. The journalists received additional fines of 100 million lei (US$9,900) each. The officer in question, however, was later dismissed from his job. (RSF)

RUSSIA

On 19 January it was announced that naval officer and journalist **Grigory Pasko** would face charges of espionage and revealing state secrets at a 'closed' military trial. A reporter for *Boyevaya Vakhta* (Battle Fleet) newspaper of the Pacific Fleet, he faces up to 20 years' imprisonment if found guilty. The nature of the trial has resulted in Pasko's lawyers being threatened with having the case taken away from them should they inform the press and public of how it is progressing. (RSF)

On 6 February **Mikhail Razgadov**, chief correspondent of the *Stolitsa-S* weekly, published in Saransk, was beaten by a department chief, Major-General Krasnoputsky, and held in the militia station for over five hours. Razgadov had been taking photos of Krasnoputsky's mansion where he was allegedly using forced labour to build private residences for himself and other officials. (Glasnost

Defence Foundation)

RWANDA

President Pascaul Bizimungu announced in mid-January that French would be replaced as the official language because of France's involvement in the 1994 genocide. (*East African, IRIN*)

Recent Publications: Gourevitch, Philip, 1998: *We Wish to Inform You That Tomorrow We Will Be Killed With Our Families: Stories From Rwanda*, Farrar Strauss & Giroux 384pp, $25.00; *Rwanda: Insurgency in north-western Rwanda*, November 1998 - Africa Rights; Howard Adelman and Astri Suhrke (eds) (to be published in 1999)*The Path of a Genocide: The Rwanda Crisis from Uganda to Zaire*, Transaction Publications Price $44.95

SERBIA-MONTENEGRO

On 4 December the Nis branch of the Serbian Socialist Party brought charges against TV5 and the editor of the programme *Raspravake* for breaking the recent Law on Public Information after they allowed representatives of the Alliance for Change, **Zoran Djindjic** and **Vesna Pesic**, and Democratic Alternative **Nebojsa Covic** to say libellous things about the authorities. Under the terms of the law, the station's management was charged with failing to react to the apparent 'insults and lies'. (B92)

On 8 December **Nikola Djuric**, general manager of City Radio in Nis, was charged

with the illegal possession and operation of a radio station, the first case in which the manager of a banned station has gone to trial. In the 18 January hearing Djuric was found guilty and sentenced to 12 months probation with a two-year suspended prison sentence. (ANEM)

On 10 December the new government-appointed dean of the School of Electronic Engineering at Belgrade University ordered the imposition of 'filters' to prevent users of the Yugoslav academic network from accessing the OpenNet web site – a major source of independent news and information. The measure also affects independent media and NGOs that access the site via the university. (HRW)

On 17 December Information Minister Aleksandar Vucic warned Albanian-language newspapers that they would be taken to court unless they changed their editorial policy. Among others, *Bujku* and *Koha Ditore* were accused of inciting the violent break of the constitutional order, territorial integrity, and of violating the rights of citizens by 'inciting national, racial and religious hatred'. On the same day, *Bujku*, the oldest Albanian paper in the region, ceased to publish after power was cut from its premises and those of its printer. (*Koha Ditore*, B92)

On 11 January journalist and chief of the Kosovo Information Centre, **Enver Malaku**, was murdered in Prishtina. (ANEM)

On 12 January inspectors of the

Yugoslav Telecommunications Ministry attempted to close Television Cacak. After inspecting the station, they passed a banning order on the grounds that the station 'did not possess a broadcasting licence'. As in other similar cases, the broadcaster had applied for a licence but had received no response from the ministry, although it was still required to pay a fee for the use of its frequency. (ANEM)

A Leskovac magistrates court imposed fines on the editor and publisher of the monthly human rights magazine *Prava coveka* (Rights of Man) on 15 January. **Bojan Toncic** was fined 50,000 dinars (approx. US$5,000) and the committee which publishes the magazine, 100,000 dinars. The charges were brought by the manager of Radio Leskovac, Zivko Ljubisavljevic, under the new Public Information Act for writing that the station deserved the praise of the ruling party for its 'tragi-comic mish-mash of silence, smoke-screen reporting and primitivism'. (B92)

On 15 January **Boban Miletic**, author of a book of aphorisms entitled *Weep Serbia, Our Motherland*, was arrested in Knjazevac. After a three-day detention he was handed to the Zajecar district attorney with a motion to charge him under Article 157 with 'exposing the state and the president to ridicule'. (ANEM)

On 18 January a police guard was stationed outside the Prishtina morgue where the bodies of 45 ethnic Albanians, killed at Racak three days earlier, were being held.

Although the guards were under orders to admit nobody other than the head of Prishtina police, a crew from Radio Television Serbia was allowed to enter. (B92)

On the night of 25 January the apartment of RTV Trstenik cameraman **Velibor Ciric** was set on fire. Ciric's family managed to escape onto the roof of the apartment, but the message 'Do not jam frequencies, switch yourself off completely' was later found inscribed on his door. (WAN)

SIERRA LEONE

On 8 December **Sulaiman Momodu**, a reporter with the independent *Concord Times* newspaper and a stringer for the BBC, was arrested by plain-clothes detectives at his residence in Freetown. He escaped from the custody of the Criminal Investigation Department (CID) and is currently being sought by police. (CPJ)

On 10 December, BBC§ reporter **Winston Ojukutu Macauley** appeared in Magistrates Court in Freetown where he was formerly charged with 'false publication' contrary to Article 98 of the Penal Code. Macauley pleaded not guilty and was released on a bail of six million leones (US$ 3,500). (CPJ)

On 11 December **Mildred Hancile**, a reporter and production assistant with SLBS, **Conrad Roy**, an editor with *Expo Times* newspaper, **Mano Mbompa Turay**, editor of the now-defunct *Eagle* newspaper

and **Amadu Jalloh**, a senior journalist with *Liberty Voice* newspaper, appeared for the first time in the magistrates' court among 22 civilians facing charges ranging from treason and aiding and abetting the enemy to conspiring to overthrow a legally constituted government. (CPJ)

On 22 December **Kabba Kargbo**, a freelance reporter with the independent newspaper *Pathfinder*, was arrested by the CID in Freetown shortly after he was interviewed by the BBC's *Focus on Africa* programmme. He had said that he had witnessed the 20 December rebel attack on nearby Waterloo and that the Revolutionary United Front (RUF) rebels appeared 'militarily superior' to the ECOMOG peacekeeping force, ECOMOG. (CPJ)

On 31 December Col. Sam Bockrie of the RUF said, during an interview with the BBC, that its Makeni stringer, **Sylvester Rogers**, was biased and that he would be 'dealt with' when the rebels captured the town. Rogers' whereabouts remain unknown. On the same day, BBC correspondents **Winston Ojukutu-Macaulay** and **Sulaiman Momodu**, were arrested again in Freetown by officers of the CID. All three were charged with 'false reporting' and 'reporting news on the war without clearing their stories in advance with the ECOMOG'. An official statement broadcast on 5 January described the journalists' actions as 'unpatriotic behavior and a criminal act which is tantamount to acting as a propagandist for the rebels'. (CPJ)

On 10 January Associated Press (AP) television producer **Myles Tierney** from New York City was killed when the vehicle he was travelling in through Freetown with others journalists was sprayed with bullets by a man reported to be a rebel. Abidjan-based AP Television West Africa bureau chief **Ian Stewart**, also in the vehicle, was shot in the head and left in critical condition. Nairobi-based AP photographer **David Guttenfelder** suffered cuts from broken glass when the station wagon was shot at. The journalists were transported and accompanied by ECOMOG soldiers and members of Ministry of Information. (CPJ)

SINGAPORE

Opposition politician **Chee Soon Juan** has been charged with breaching the Public Entertainments Act for making a speech without a permit. If convicted he faces a penalty of US$3,000 in fines and a five-year ban on running for office. Chee spoke about government accountability to several hundred people in the central business district on 29 December. As he took the witness stand on 1 February, Chee challenged his prosecutors, arguing that his speech constituted 'a very serious talk with my fellow citizens' and so had little to do with public entertainment. Under the Act, permission is required for all public events. In court, police Superintendent Low Hui Hui testified that unregulated speeches could lead to a

breakdown of law and order. His fears were dismissed by defence lawyer Joshua Jeyaretnam who considered the odds of this happening was the same 'as Martians invading Singapore'. (CNN)

SOLOMON ISLANDS

On 18 January the *Solomon Star* began publishing seven days a week, making it the first daily newspaper in the islands' history. (Pacific Island Report, Pacnews)

On 2 February, the provincial assembly caucus on Guadalcanal has asked the minister responsible for the media to ban further statements about growing ethnic tension on the island. The media ban would include statements from Police Commissioner **Frank Short**, who told the national radio service that he would not be stopped from presenting the truth about the situation. (Pacific Islands News Association)

SPAIN

In January a group of Basque journalists announced the launch of *Oihartzuna* (Echo) an Internet publication aimed at promoting Basque issues. The two specific areas of concern are conditions in which prisoners are kept in both French and Spanish gaols and the lack of output for wider Basque issues since the closure in July of the daily *Egin* (*Index* 5/1998). (*Oihartzuna Aldizkaria*)

SRI LANKA

In early December the government replaced the deputy

Chief of Staff of the Army as the 'competent authority' for censorship on war news. Ariya Rubasinghe, director of the government's information department, said that he would relax the rules for the foreign media but not for domestic outlets. Formal censorship was reimposed last June (*Index* 4/1998, 6/1998). (Reuters)

On 4 January charges were filed before the Colombo High Court against two air force officers in connection with the attempted abduction of journalist **Iqbal Athas** in February 1998 (*Index* 2/1998, 4/1998). The men were charged with unlawful entry and threathening Athas at gunpoint. (AI)

On 14 January the police sought a court order to exhume an alleged mass graves site in the northern Jaffna peninsula. It was the first concrete step taken since it said that it would investigate a soldier's claims that he could identify where up to 400 Tamils had been buried after being murdered by government forces (*Index* 5/1998, 6/1998). (Voice of America)

On 28 January reports indicated that Internal and International Commerce and Food Minister Kingsley T. Wickremaratne and Agriculture and Lands Minister and Peoples Alliance General Secretary D. M. Jayaratne were planning to sue the Centre for Monitoring Election Violence (CMEV) for criminal defamation. The ministers allege that there is a conspiracy between the CMEV and the official opposition to tarnish the government's 'victory' in the 25 January North West province elections. CMEV has called for the election to be annulled because the violent election campaign did not provide a climate for a free and fair election. (Reuters, Centre for Monitoring Election Violence, *Daily News*)

The house of **M. W. Somaratne**, provincial reporter for the daily *Lankadeepa*, was attacked and severely damaged by unknown individuals on 28 January. The attack took place after he wrote items supporting government policies during the recent North West Province election campaign. (RSF)

On 1 February the government banned satellite phones from the war zone in the north and east of the country. US satellite phone company Iridium was given a licence to operate its service, but only in the central and southern regions. Extension of coverage to the war zone was opposed by the Ministry of Defence because it did not want the Liberation Tigers of Tamil Eelam to have greater access to global communications. (Agence France Presse)

On 4 February diplomats in Colombo claimed that the Foreign Ministry had told them to keep their mouths shut about the conduct of the 25 January North West Provincial poll, and that any further public comments on the matter would be considered interference in the country's internal affairs. (Reuters, Voice of America)

Recent publication: *Scarred Minds: the Psychological Impact of* *War on Sri Lankan Tamils* (Sage, 1998, pp 352); *Fifty Years On: Censorship, conflict and media reform in Sri Lanka* (Article XIX, December 1998, pp 70). ´

In early December two Catholic priests, **Hillary Boma** and **Lina Tujano**, were charged with exploding a dozen bombs in Khartoum on 30 June. The two, and their 18 co-defendants, face death by crucifixion if found guilty of an alleged plot to mar celebrations marking the anniversary of the 1998 coup which brought the National Islamic Front to power. The trial, which began at army headquarters in October, has been denounced as a charade based on confessions extracted under torture. Foreign journalists and diplomats have been barred. (*Washington Post, Guardian*)

Recent Publications: Zwier, Lawrence J, 1998 *Sudan: North Against South (World in Conflict)* Lerner Publications; *Food and power in Sudan – A Critique of Humanitarianism* (African Rights, May 1997 372pp)

On 13 January, the newspapers *Jumhuriyat, Khalq Ovozi* and the Russian-language *Narodnaya Gazeta* were brought under the control of the executive staff of the president. The Ministry of Communications will be responsible for their distribution, via subscription and retail outlets. The purpose of the takeover is 'make it easier to inform the public about state policy'. (SWB)

Journalists **A Vokhidov** and **S Dostiev**, editors-in-chief of the closed newspapers *Istiklol* and *Samar*, faced the prospect of criminal trial for libel in mid-January. The pair are accused of defaming Kurbonali Mirzoaliev, chairman of the executive committee of Vosey district and a parliamentary deputy, in an article the two newspapers published two years ago. Mirzoaliev has already succeeded in having the article's authors prosecuted for criminal libel. (Glasnost Defence Foundation)

Chombeza, a Swahili-language tabloid, was banned on 8 December for allegedly publishing a photograph which showed an individual's private parts. Information Minister Mohammed Seif Khatib said the ban was 'in conformity' with social values and would save children and the youth from 'falling prey to contemptuous and pornographic cartoons'. (*Guardian*, MISA)

Police on 8 December prevented **Ali Sultan**, a *Daily Mail* freelance journalist, from covering a treason trial at the Vuga magistrate's court in Zanzibar. Some 10 armed policemen were reported to have escorted the journalist to an exit even though he had shown them his press card. The police claimed that the reporter's bench was full and 'there is no more space for journalists'. Journalists who attended the session denied that the bench was full. (MISA)

President Salmin Almour of

Zanzibar on 18 January lifted the ban imposed on two mainland dailies, *Majira* and *Mtanzania*. (MISA).

TONGA

On 8 February *Tonga Times* publisher and editor **Kalafi Moala** was ordered to pay US$25,360 in damages to Minister of Police Clive Edwards. Edwards sued the newspaper over an article published last January alleging that the minister was at the forefront of the government's persecution of its political rivals. (Pacnews, Radio Tonga)

TUNISIA

Taoufik Ben Brick, a correspondent with the French press agency SYFIA, has been once again the victim of intimidation tactics and telephone threats. On 28 January five men vandalised his car and also made off with a child's car seat to represent it as a robbery attempt. On the same day he received threatening telephone calls from the secret service. Ben Brick had recently written an article concerning bread subsidies, a strategic commodity in Tunisia (*Index* 5/1998). (RSF)

TURKEY

Five police officers accused of the murder of **Metin Goktepe** (*Index* 2/1996, 1/1997, 6/1997, 1/1998, 2/1998, 3/1998, 5/1998, 1/1999) were temporarily released on 11 December. Human rights organisations expressed concern as key witnesses to the murder have, in the past, been subject to

pressures and threats, often from police circles. (RSF)

On 18 December journalist **Nuredin Sirin**, an editor with the Islamic daily *Selam*, was sentenced to a 20-month prison term for an article on 15 July last year entitled 'One has to side with the oppressed, even if they are atheists'. The journalist outlined his views on the Kurdish question. (RSF)

The government lodged an official complaint with Switzerland after the Basle Cable Network (BCN) on 6 January replaced broadcasts of Turkish state-run television TRT with the Kurdish-language channel Med-TV (*Index* 2/1997, 5/1997, 6/1998, 1/1999). The BCN says it launched Med-TV because of popular demand (Reuters)

On 4 January the newspaper *Yeni Evrensel* (Universal News) was banned from distribution in the Emergency Region of south-east Anatolia. Since 1 December 1997, the pro-Kurdish daily *Ulkede Gundem* is also banned in those areas. (IMK)

Dr Cumhar Akpinar, a doctor at the Ankara State Institute of Forensic Medicine, has been detained by police since 15 January for reporting cases of police torture of detainees. (Human Rights Foundation)

The Supreme Board of Radio and Television (RTUK), which patrols national and local broadcasting, issued a total of 286 penalties to private radio and television stations during 1998 but none to TRT's string

of state-owned stations. (Washington Kurdish Institute)

The first issue of the bi-monthly journal *Jin u Jiyan* (Women and Life), published by a Kurdish women's centre in Istanbul, was confiscated on orders of the State Security Court on 16 January. (IMK)

Two trade unionists from the south-east region of Elazig, **Resul Alinak** and **Mehmet Cakan**, were charged in January with organising a cultural event where songs were sung in Kurdish, a prohibited language. (IMK)

Ozgur Cebe, the Diyarbakir representative of the newspaper *Yeni Evrensel*, was detained by police in the south east region of 25 January. He was released later the same day. (Campaign For Human Rights In Turkey)

On 9 February **Sanar Yurdatapan** (*Index* 3/1997, 3/1998, 5/1998, 6/1998), the human rights defender and organiser of the 'Initiative for Peace in Turkey', was sentenced to two months in jail for an interview he published with two army deserters. Yurdatapan, son of a famous general, refused as a civilian to answer any questions put by a court martial and stressed the incompatibility of Turkish laws with international agreements and conventions. (*Kurdistan Observer*)

TURKMENISTAN

Vyacheslav Mamedov, a leader of the Russian community in the Caspian Sea port of Turkmenbashi, was detained on 21 January and

SAPURMURAT NIYAZOV

Flattery: a dental expert speaks

How are you getting on, lads, on the eve of the New Year, and how is your spirit? Well then, please tell me about your plans and problems. I want to hear them... Feature and publicity films are good, but you have been showing a lot of them lately. Most of them praise the president and are about the president. You must know one thing: if you eat sweets all the time, then you will lose the taste for them. Even if a child eats sweets all the time, he will end up with cavities and lose his teeth. You have to know the limit for each thing... I would like you to analyse how people accept your broadcasts about the president. I know that you mean well. Do not look at me, but look at the people and see how they see it.

Your [radio] broadcast is very poor. You must like your job. You must assess your broadcast on the basis of how it will influence people. You have no idea about it. Your broadcasts must have the proper influence on the people and the country... This is not the way to do the job – only praising the president. When I start listening to the morning music programme, it becomes difficult for me, and my heart bleeds when I listen to all this 'Turkmen president' and 'Turkmenbashi' at 7:15 in the morning after the news programme. It is all right for one or two days but... Your evening news is also no good.

President Saparmurat Niyazov criticised the extremity of the praise lavished on him by Turkmen Television and Radio in a meeting on 21 December. Parliament has awarded Niyazov the title Turkmenbashi, the father of all the Turkmen, and his giant portrait graces banknotes, town squares, factories and hospitals. Translated from a broadcast on Turkmen state television by BBC Monitoring.

taken to Ashkhabad for questioning by agents of the Committee for National Security (CNS). Mamedov's detention relates to an interview he gave to the Russian radio station Mayak that was later branded 'defamatory'. (Glasnost Defence Foundation)

UGANDA

On 17 December **George Lugalambi**, editor of the *Crusader*, and **Meddie Musisi**, a reporter with the paper, were detained at Kampala police station for interrogation. Lugalambi was later charged with 'promoting sectarianism' in an article. He was released on bail and his passport confiscated by the court. Musisi was released without charge. (CPJ)

James Mujone, a journalist with the privately owned *New Vision*, was on 19 December arrested in Mbarara and taken to Kampala where he was questioned over unspecified articles published in the newspaper and which the authorities categorised as 'incitement'. (CPJ).

UNITED KINGDOM

On 3 December **Tony Geraghty**, a former journalist known for writing about the security forces, was arrested by Ministry of Defence police under the Official Secrets Act. Geraghty was arrested under a clause that permits the government to detain journalists receiving confidential information. His book *The Irish War* details covert operations and surveillance tactics used by the SAS and MI5 in Northern

Ireland. (*Guardian*)

The House of Lords ruled on the 18 December to overturn an earlier decision that General Augusto Pinochet did not enjoy sovereign immunity from prosecution (*Index* 1/1999). The ruling came after Pinochet's lawyers challenged the original ruling on the grounds that Lord Hoffmann, who cast the deciding vote, had not declared an affiliation to Amnesty International. Conservative MPs called for Hoffmann to resign after flouting the principle that justice 'must be seen to be done'. (*Guardian, Daily Telegraph, Financial Times*)

The Press Complaints Commission ruled on 8 January that the *Guardian* was not guilty of 'inaccuracies and misleading statements' in a July 1998 article that examined public apprehension about genetically modified food produced by the US biotech company Monsanto. (*Guardian*)

On January 10 it was reported that Home Secretary Jack Straw had unveiled plans to consider accepting hearsay evidence in trials of drug dealers and sex offenders, because of the alarming number of cases dropped on the grounds of witness intimidation. (*Daily Telegraph*)

On 27 January Channel 5 issued a statement refusing to change its stance on screening late-night erotic dramas. A spokesman said that it was hypocritical to say that it was 'all right to show erotic scenes if in a dramatic context or on pay television'. (*Guardian*)

The England football manager **Glenn Hoddle** sparked a major row on 31 January in an interview with Matt Dickinson of *The Times* in which he said that people with disabilities were paying the price for sins they had committed in a past life. The statement caused a furore, with disabled rights groups and politicians, including Prime Minister Tony Blair, calling on Hoddle to resign. Lord Ashley, a disabled rights campaigner, said that he thought Hoddle's opinions were hurtful, but he did not believe 'he should be sacked for his opinions'. Hoddle resigned on 3 February. (*Guardian, Daily Telegraph*)

The debate over genetically modified (GM) food escalated in mid-February when a discredited report, which resulted in the suspension of a respected Hungarian scientist, was found to contain valid findings about the degeneration of the intestines of rats after eating GM potatoes. Some 20 international scientists signed a latter of protest at the suppression of the research of Dr **Arpad Pusztai** at Rowett Research Institute near Aberdeen, who was gagged with the threat of losing his pension rights. As politicians sought to allay public fears, it emerged that an article written 'spontaneously' in defence of the new food proved to have been commissioned from Professor Jonathan Jones, an employee of the laboratory set up by Lord Sainsbury, the government Food Minister, a majority shareholder in one of the UK's leading retail chains and a gene patent-holder. Sainsbury denied any influence

SIR KEITH THOMAS
Sheer poetry

It has been said that the amount of money saved by giving up contemporary poetry was too small to justify dropping the list. But, for a publisher like Oxford University Press (OUP), contemporary poetry has a high opportunity cost, involving, as it does, a diversion of managerial time, capital and marketing resources from our core activities. Giving up the contemporary poetry list, like giving up other parts of the trade list, is painful for OUP, but it is necessary both practically and symbolically. It means reasserting our strategic priorities and accepting that we cannot be good at everything. It is an earnest of Oxford's intention to concentrate on those parts of the business which are integral to its purpose, and to make them commercially successful. There will always be a tension between financial and academic priorities. But it is certain that a reduction in the Press' commercial effectiveness would diminish its academic effectiveness as well. OUP has a responsibility, to its staff, its customers, its authors and its owners, to concentrate on what it can do best. One of the subjects it does well is contemporary music. OUP's music department has over 20 people who specialise in publishing and promoting the music repertoire, and their is a flourishing business: whereas the rights income from OUP's contemporary poetry list was between £3,000 and £6,000 a year, that from contemporary music list is in hundreds of thousands.

Sir Keith Thomas *is President of Corpus Christi College, Oxford, and Chairman of the Delegates' Finance Committee of Oxford University Press which, in November 1998, announced that it was dropping its contemporary poetry list (Index 1/1999). The above passage was extracted from a right of reply published in the* Times Literary Supplement *on 5 February 1999.*

over decisions about GM, saying he left the room every time that the subject was raised in cabinet meetings. (*Daily Telegraph, Gaudian, Observer*)

On 20 January Home Secretary Jack Straw obtained a High Court injunction preventing the *Sunday Telegraph* from reporting leaked extracts of a report into the murder of black London teenager, Stephen Lawrence. The injunction was obtained after the first editions of the paper had gone on sale and other news organisations had already reported on *Telegraph's* article. Straw argued that partial leaking would be 'profoundly unfair' not only to the family of Stephen Lawrence but also to the Metropolitan Police which the report accused of systemic racism. However, on 21 January various news organisations and civil liberties groups announced their intention to challenge Mr Justice Rix's ruling. Following hours of sustained pressure, the Home Office agreed to change the wording of the injunction to allow reporting on extracts of the report already in the public domain. (*The Times, Guardian, Telegraph*)

USA

On 9 December ABC-TV's 20/20 aired an interview with Leonard Weinglass, an attorney for **Mumia Abu-Jamal**, the activist and former radio journalist who is on death row for killing a Philadelphia police officer (*Index* 2/1995, 6/1995, 2/1996, 6/1996, 1/1997). The day after the segment was aired, Weinglass told *CounterSpin*: 'They would not accept anything I said in over one hour

of an on-camera interview, and instead just took snippets here and there and interspersed them with refutations from the prosecution and from prosecutor representatives and police officers.' (A-Infos News Service).

On the first weekend in January a car was driven through the a steel gate and set on fire in front of a building in Queens, New York, that housed Media Marketing Research Incorporated, a New York company that distributes the international Arabic newspaper *Al Hayat*. Two days earlier, an unidentified caller left a threatening message on the company's answering machine. (*New York Times*)

A new postage stamp, featuring the late American artist **Jackson Pollock**, will soon be issued. The image, taken from a 1949 photograph, has been doctored to remove the cigarette dangling from his lips. (*Daily Telegraph*)

A topless woman, who appears for a fifteenth of a second on two frames of Disney's *The Rescuers*, has forced the company to recall more than 3 million copies of the recently released video. The image, which cannot be seen by the naked eye, was removed from versions shown in cinemas in the 1970s, but was overlooked in the video version. Apparently, the nude was inserted by the animators as a joke when they made the master copy. (*Daily Telegraph*)

On 14 January California's Alameda County Superior Court dismissed a lawsuit seeking to require the

Livermore Library to censor Internet use. The ruling marks the second time the court has rejected an attempt to force the library to abandon its open-access policy governing Internet use. A similar case in Virginia was struck down in November (*Index* 1/1999). (ACLU)

On 25 January **Timothy Boomer** appeared in a Michigan district court, accused of using indecent language in the presence of women and children. Boomer was ticketed on 15 August for cursing while standing in the Rifle River after falling out of his canoe. He had violated an 1897 ordinance which makes it a misdemeanour to 'use any indecent, immoral, obscene, vulgar or insulting language in the presence or hearing of any woman or child' under penalty of imprisonment for up to 90 days. (ACLU)

On 28 January a row at NBC erupted over whether to broadcast reporter **Lisa Myers'** interview with a woman who claims to have been raped by President Clinton in 1978 at the Camelot Hotel in Little Rock, Arkansas. In an affidavit prepared during the Paula Jones case, the woman denied any sexual encounter, but later told the FBI during the Kenneth Starr investigation that her affidavit was 'false'. (*Daily Telegraph*)

On 2 February a Philadelphia judge blocked a law to prevent website operations from making sexually explicit materials available to under-17s. In his ruling, Judge Lowell Reed said: 'While the public certainly has an interest in protecting its minors, the public interest is not served by the enforcement of an unconstitutional law. Indeed, perhaps we do the minors of this country great harm if First Amendment protections, which they will with age inherit fully, are chipped away in the name of their protection.' (*Guardian*)

On 4 February US District Judge Nina Gershon dismissed a 1995 lawsuit against Nassau County Community College for its course on 'Human Sexuality and Family Life'. The plaintiffs argued that the course was unconstitutional because it violated the separation of church and state. Gershon ruled that religious groups should not dictate curriculum on public campuses. (Freedom Forum)

UZBEKISTAN

On 13 January the authorities blocked reception of BBC programmes by moving the broadcasts to much less accessible frequencies. Yuri Goligorsky, the BBC's chief editor of broadcasting in Central Asia and the Caucasus, said the corporation's programming 'had been taken off the air'. (RSF)

VIETNAM

General **Tran Do**, who once served as head of ideology for the Commission for Culture, Literature and Arts, was expelled from the Communist Party on 8 January for publicly criticising the party. Last year he wrote a series of letters urging major political reform and criticising corruption, inefficient state-owned industries and increased restrictions on freedom of expression. (Associated Press)

ZAMBIA

On 25 November, police briefly detained the Zambian correspondent for South Africa's Channel Africa Radio, **Mweene Miyanda**, after she interviewed one of the 1997 coup suspects on trial for treason. Miyanda was picked up at the High Court when she allegedly interviewed opposition Zambia Democratic Congress president Dean Mung'omba in the courtroom. (MISA)

On 1 December, scores of supporters of opposition presidential aspirant Anderson Mazoka stormed the Livingstone bureau offices of the *Zambia Daily Mail* in protest at a lead story which linked Mazoka to Satanism, reports the private *Post* newspaper. The *Mail* carried a story titled 'Devil's club exposed', which reported that Mazoka once admitted to being a Freemason. Mazoka's supporters demanded to see *Zambia Daily Mail* bureau chief and author of the story, **George Malunga**, but he had fled the building. (MISA).

Information Minister Newstead Zimba said on 9 December that the independent *Post* newspaper's presence on the Internet is 'splashing a wrong impression of Zambia all over the world through irresponsible reporting'. 'One would think these people (the *Post*) belong to another country,' he said. (MISA)

The High Court on 28 January fined Inspector General of Police Francis Ndhlovu one million kwacha (US$400) for failing to appear at a hearing in which he is being sued by the independent *Post*. Ndhlovu, along with the Zambia Telecommunications Company (ZAMTEL) and the attorney general, have been cited as respondents in a civil suit initiated by editor-in-chief of the *Post* **Fred M'membe** for illegal tapping of the newspaper's telephones two years ago. (MISA)

Compiled by: John Kamau, Regina Jere-Malanda, Daniel Rogers (Africa); Rupert Clayton, Andrew Kendle, Ruth Pilch, Catherine Richards (Asia); Simon Martin (eastern Europe and CIS); Dolores Cortés (south and central America); Arif Azad, Gill Newsham, Neil Sammonds (Middle East); Billie Felix Jeyes (north America and Pacific); Tony Callaghan (UK and western Europe).

MELANIE FRIEND

Kosovo: home and away

Kosovo Feb 1999: Charred remains of a village near
Podujevo

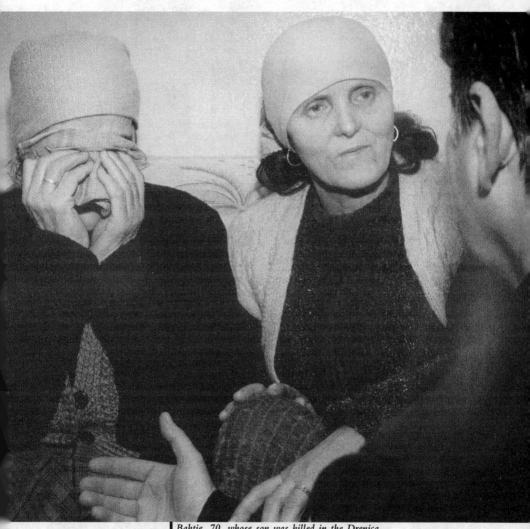

Bahtie, 70, whose son was killed in the Drenica region, and Sevdije, her 42-year-old cousin whose husband was also killed, talk to a woman's 'activist' helping women and children traumatised and displaced by the war in an Albanian women's centre, mostly from the Drenica region

Kosovar/Albanian asylum seekers in the UK. A dormitory in the emergency accomodation shelter provided for refugees by Barking & Dagenham Council in autumn 1998. The refugees were later housed in B&B accommodation or flats

Early morning, a house in Pristina. Albanian girls and young women (aged 12-22), displaced from their shelled village near Podujevo, in hiding with relatives in Pristina. Fifteen of them have slept in this one room for the last two months. When they fled their homes during the shelling, they left their ID cards behind; now they dare not leave the house, as to be stopped by police without an ID is very dangerous

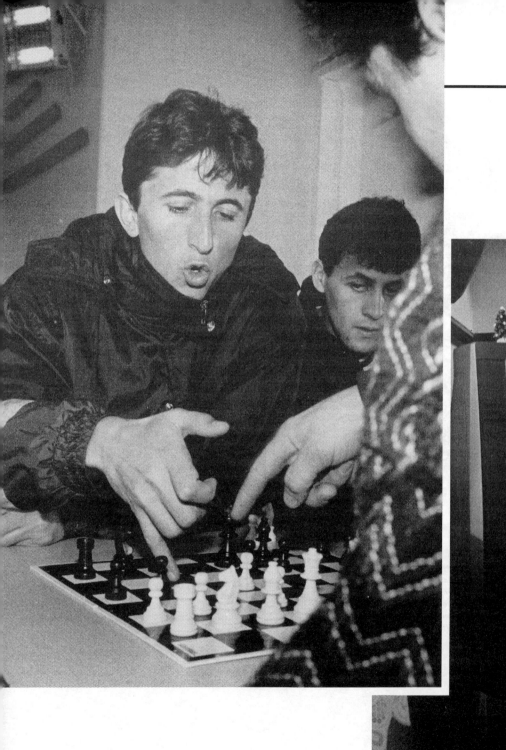

The Ripple Hall community centre in Barking, UK, where Albanian refugees can get hot food and while away some time

Hamide, who arrived in England in 1994 after her family were shot at by Serbs, with her 3-year-old son Gentrit, watch a video showing members of their family in Kosova. ❏

SUSAN WHITFIELD

In praise of the plagiarist

Up to the modern era censorship remained less of a threat to the survival of books, than accidental loss and destruction in fires, rebellions and wars

A scholar of the sixth century AD enumerated five bibliothetical catastrophes in Chinese history, starting with the book burning of 221BC. In fact, far more than five major libraries had been destroyed by this time, but only the first was the result of a deliberate policy. The rest, like the fire at Alexandria, were accidental. One reason for the numerous catastrophes was that 'China' did not have a single library equivalent to that of Alexandria, but a whole succession, each larger than the last. Scholars, and the state itself, were consummate librarians from earliest times.

The earliest examples of state archives date from the second millennium BC and consist of the 'oracle bones' used by court diviners to answer the king's questions. It is probable that bamboo and wood were used for other records, but none are extant from this period. By the first millennium BC, texts were inscribed on stone and bronze and, a little later, silk came into use. 'History,' a contemporary text notes, 'is too important a matter to be left to memory.'

The states' libraries included philosophy, *belles lettres*, manuals and, in a later era, canonical Buddhist and Daoist texts. In 408BC, when the state of Wei defeated Zhongshan, the general insisted on taking all the credit for the victory. To dampen his pretensions the king ordered the archivist to bring out two chests of books, all treatises on the strategy used in attacking Zhongshan. The size of state archives in early times is not known, but the fact that Wei had two chests of books on one subject

圖　架　書

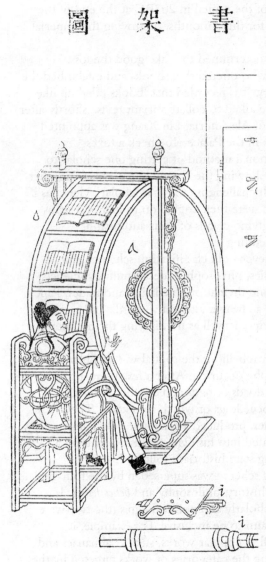

Qindong gujin tushu jicheng (Synthesis of books and illustrations of ancient and modern times) compiled by imperial order and printed in 1726 in copper movable type.
British Library 15023.b.1

suggests that they were considerable. For the state, knowledge of the past was the means to control the present. In 527BC, the King of Qin chided one of his officials: 'As a descendant of the state archivist of Qin, how can you be so ignorant?' He warned that his name would be lost to posterity because of this lack of historical knowledge. Three centuries later, a Qin king declared himself the first emperor and ordered the destruction of many texts he considered to be subversive, but he excluded the Qin annals.

After each bibliothetical catastrophe, the substantial private libraries were searched for replacements. The philosopher Mozi (fourth century BC) travelled with five cartloads of books, and the tomb of a third-century scholar contained books 'sufficient to fill scores of carts'. Unfortunately these private libraries also fell victim to the destruction by rebels which often accompanied the fall of a dynasty. Thus the Qin emperor's deliberate act of book burning was far less destructive than the burning of the capital in 207BC at the end of the Qin dynasty. The fires blazed for three months, destroying the imperial collection.

Emperor Wu (140–87BC) determined to make good the loss. He promised rewards to scholars who offered their books and established the first centralised imperial library. It is recorded that 'books piled up like hills' and leading scholars were asked to collate variant texts. Shortly after the destruction of the library of Alexandria, Liu Xiang was appointed Collator of Secret Documents in the Palace. To check a text's authenticity he used the traditional method of getting one scholar to check and emend it and then showing the emended passages to another scholar, who was charged with challenging the first scholar's views 'as if he were his enemy'. The texts were then copied on to bamboo strips and a catalogue was written, giving details of their authorship, significance and notes on the editing.

Liu Xiang's son devised a seven-fold classification scheme: general works, the six Confucian classics, philosophy, poetry, military science, astronomy and mathematics, and divination, medicine and trades. Paper now came into use, providing a cheaper alternative to silk and a more convenient one to bamboo strips, as well as multiplying the number of books in circulation.

In AD24 there was another rebellion; the capital was set ablaze, and another bibliothetical catastrophe occurred. After a few years, private libraries had yielded 2,000 cartloads of texts and another scholarly convention was called, the proceedings of which are extant. Their author, the state historiographer, produced a catalogue of the imperial collection which he incorporated into his dynastic history, setting a precedent which all succeeding state historians followed.

The seven-fold cataloguing scheme was superseded by the four-fold one still in use today: classics, history, philosophy and *belles lettres*. It reflected the interests of the scholarly and political elites (the two were largely the same) and did not aim to be inclusive. For example, it omitted religious books as well as popular works, such as almanacs and divination texts. These last were the categories of works targeted by the first censorship laws in the third century AD. There were sound political reasons why the emperor wished to restrict access to such texts: they could predict the end of a dynasty and had been used as an ideological justification by rebels throughout history. Chinese libraries were therefore great preservers of orthodox texts and deliberate excluders of texts considered heterodox.

Even before heterodox works were actively banned, the fact that they were of no interest to scholars had serious consequences. Many works were lost because they were neither in imperial nor private collections, and scholars did not bother to transmit them. Even worse, whereas we know the titles of many lost books included in the bibliographies, we have no record of lost books not included. Fortunately, as well as being great collectors and cataloguers, scholars were also avid plagiarists and anthologisers. It has, therefore, been possible to reconstruct large parts of some lost texts from quotations found in other works.★

Anthologising began in ancient times: the *Book of Odes*, part of the Confucian canon, is an anthology of folk songs collected in the first millennium BC. Literary anthologies were made from the fourth century AD, and became basic readers for scholars sitting the civil service examinations. The earliest collections of complete books started in the thirteenth century and culminated with the *Four Treasuries*, initiated in 1772 and distinguished by being by far the most comprehensive and well-enforced act of censorship in Chinese history to that point. Officials scoured the empire for texts, to determine which were subversive and to destroy them, along with their printing blocks, or to edit out the offending passages.

The final anthology of 3,460 works in 79,339 volumes was printed in eight sets, of which two are more or less extant. It is both a tremendous literary achievement as well as a terrible reminder of what had been. No single list of banned works survives, but a review of the various lists shows 2,320 works listed for total suppression and over 300 for partial suppression, including the works of major literary figures who were considered political subversives, loyal to the previous Ming dynasty rather than the Qing Manchu regime. Some banned works survive, either because they were taken to Japan or were in private libraries which were left untouched, notably those of Manchu bibliophiles and Christian missionaries. But many others are no longer extant.

Paternalism motivated censorship throughout Chinese history, from the book burning of the first emperor to the selection under the Qianlong emperor two millennia later. In both cases, trusted scholars were allowed to retain their private collections intact, proving that the emperor did not consider knowledge dangerous *per se* but only when in the wrong hands – those of potential rebels, be they disgruntled Confucian officials, Ming dynasty loyalists or, in the case of the frequent banning of divination texts, the less well-educated.

The monastery library was a third important source of books, keeping Confucian classics and literary works as well as Buddhist scriptures. The cave library in Dunhuang, Central Asia, is the only extant collection of a Buddhist library from the first millennium and includes the earliest dated printed book in the world, the *Diamond Sutra* dated 868AD, showing the importance of Buddhism on the development of printing. A ninth century almanac, also in the cave, was printed illegally by a family firm in the capital itself. Such a flagrant disregard of the censorship laws – and this is not an isolated example – can only suggest that they were not strictly enforced.

The reverence with which Chinese scholars regarded books is shown in numerous examples of their super-human efforts to preserve libraries during their lifetimes. One scholar tried to protect his library even after death, appending colophons to his books warning descendants that to lose or sell them would be an act contrary to filial piety. But bibliothetical catastrophes continued throughout Chinese history, destroying countless thousands of works. It is no longer possible to know or to reconstruct many of these, but the untiring efforts of emperors and scholars have meant that ancient China has nevertheless bequeathed us a rich literary legacy. ❏

* I am indebted to Professor Glen Dudbridge of Oxford University for these insights. He will be giving the Panizzi Lectures at the British Library on lost Chinese books in the autumn.

Dr Susan Whitfield runs the International Dunhuang Project at the British Library, working on manuscripts from the Dunhuang library. She is also preparing a history of censorship in China and will be lecturing at the Censorship Summer School in Cambridge in August.

MICHAEL HOLROYD

Places of opportunity

Public libraries have always offered a second chance for those who missed out on formal education: now that safety net is threatened

Unlike many of my contemporaries, I never went to a university. I went instead to the Maidenhead Public Library, a mile or so from where I lived. Maidenhead had an excellent public library. It was characteristic of my family that they should have taken this for granted. Everyone did. But they would have complained indignantly if anyone proposed pulling it down. It was free, of course, in the sense that borrowing books was free. Everyone approved of that in those days. But it was also not free, in the sense that it had to be paid for out of the rates. No one liked paying rates, but even here there was a general agreement, an all-party agreement, that public libraries were one of the good things that came from paying our rates. What happy days they were!

Maidenhead Public Library was typical of the best sort of medium-sized public library that flourished in Britain in the 1950s and 1960s. Although I had no money and no obvious prospects, I commanded there magnificent rows of shelves stuffed with classics from the past as well as the latest publications I saw reviewed in the newspapers. I used this library as if it were my own — which, in a non-exclusive sense, it was. I might not know any writers, but I had their works whenever I wanted them. I might not know any editors, but I read their magazines. And I had warmth and light and reasonable comfort in which to read, pursue my education and enjoy myself. The Maidendead Public Library became my gentleman's club, my home-from-home, my university. Nor do I think my experience was unique. All over the country, people were using public libraries in much the same way. They provided, and to some extent I believe still provide, the continuing education of the people. They are open to all of us: children, students and the unemployed; to companies as well as individuals; and to writers such as myself – for I still regulary use my public library in London.

I remember Brigid Brophy calculating in the 1970s that there were more books taken out of public libraries in Britain in a year than there were football tickets bought for the English and Scottish league games. Such a startling statistic illustrates the fact that, though often uncelebrated, the public library was, and still is, one of the most popular institutions in Britain.

Looking back, I don't think it would have been possible for me to begin writing without this centre for learning and enjoyment – a centre that gave access not only to information but also to works of imagination. I owe the public library system an immense debt of gratitude. It has been invaluable to me.

Public libraries nourish and support what Dr Johnson called 'the common reader'. It was due to the great increase in literacy that, some 70 years after Johnson's death, the first public libraries were established in Canterbury, Warrington and Salford under the old Museum Act; and a library was opened in Brighton after a private act of parliament. That was all within two or three years of 1850. That year, too, saw the passing (against stiff opposition) of the Public Libraries Act which empowered borough councils with a population of 10,000 in England, Wales and subsequently Scotland, to spend a halfpenny rate – around one fifth of a penny at today's rate, or about USc3 – on libraries and museums. A halfpenny was not perhaps generous, but then public libraries are not accustomed to overflowing state generosity. This rate did two things: it established a principle and at the same time imposed severe restrictions on putting this principle into practice – a very English compromise.

Anyone who has been engaged in a campaign involving books, from the struggle to change copyright and the 'Thirty Years' War', to introduce Public Lending Right, to the battle against the imposition of VAT on books and the fight against the privatisation of public libraries, will not be surprised to learn how achingly slow was the progress of the public library movement in Britain. In 1855, the rate was raised to one penny; in 1855 the population limit was removed. Gradually, round the country, public libraries began to open: first at Winchester, then

Alsop and Störmer's model for proposed library in Peckham, London
— Credit: Roderick Cayne

Manchester and, after that, Liverpool, Sheffield, Birmingham and Norwich. But from 1857 to 1885 London itself had only one public library – in Westminster. The Library Association came into being in 1877 and, by the end of the century, there were some 400 public libraries in Britain. Yet, even after World War I, they were still intensely controversial places. Their supporters believed they would encourage refinement, thrift, sobriety and other allied virtues among the working classes. Their opponents objected to the burden on the rates and argued that all this promiscuous reading would lead to idleness, depravity and revolution. It was not so different from the debate on television and sex in recent times. Many people seemed to believe that unprotected free reading was deeply injurious to health.

The development of public libraries over 60 years was undoubtedly slowed down by public parsimony – a public parsimony that was put to shame by the private generosity of men such as Andrew Carnegie. It is not to our credit that Britain's public libraries came to rely so largely on a US philanthropist. Even before World War I, Carnegie had donated well over £2,000 (over US$5,000 at the time) – an extraordinary amount for those days. By the mid-1920s, with the help of the Carnegie Trust, most counties had started a good library service. Rumours that the private libraries traditionally used by the middle-classes – such as those run by Boots the Chemist, where you could pick up a romance or thriller with your soap and toothpaste – were ending their days, were already in the air.

It is worth remembering that, despite the depression of the early 1930s, local spending on public libraries actually rose between the end of the 1920s and the end of the 1930s from £1.8m to £3.2m. And this expansion persisted after World War II. Today, with their brilliant new technology, the wonderful provision for children, the exhibitions of pictures, the live readings by poets, novelists, playwrights and even the odd biographer, as well as the lending of music in various forms, public libraries have transformed themselves.

Nevertheless there are genuine fears that this narrative of hard-won success is being interrupted or halted altogether – perhaps even put into reverse. The recent recession, unlike the one in the 1930s, put the public library system under special threat. Its purchasing power has plummeted in comparison with the price and quantity of books published, and some libraries have been obliged to buy no new fiction – the category of book that is loaned more than any other. Though it is true that more than 300 new libraries opened in the 1980s, others have closed and we have seen diminishing opening hours. Such changes, and the widespread belief that libraries are deteriorating, have prompted some anxious questioning. Does the common reader, as Dr Johnson first saw him and Virginia Woolf later envisioned her, still exist? Do books hold the same place in Britain as they did in the first half of this century? Has the monopoly of the written word been broken by radio and television, and does this signal the end of reading? The fact is that we publish far more today than we did 50 years ago, but is this a symptom of panic-inflation rather than real productivity? Has the Waterstone's revolution in our bookshops adversely affected our public libraries? Why do recent surveys show that the income of authors is drastically below the national average?

Of course changes in information storage and retrieval are affecting libraries. There are extraordinary developments along the superhighways and within the brave new world of the Internet. But that magical hinged object, the book, which works from the computer in your head, has remarkable staying power. The death of the public library has been reported as many times as the death of the novel. But the novel persists because it depends on the need of readers to make their own imaginative pictures rather than simply receive uniform images on screens. The reader converts what is read into a personal experience. Similarly, public libraries will continue to exist not simply as zones for remote access to information, or as 'venues' to be 'targeted' with education. They are places of refuge and opportunity, places where raw information can be turned into knowledge, places where our imaginations may be awakened, and anything can happen. I am a product of my time at the Maidenhead Public Library, and I know. ❏

Michael Holroyd is the biographer of Lytton Strachey and George Bernard Shaw, and is presently writing an autobiography, Basil Street Blues *(Little Brown, Octover 1999). He is chairman of the Royal Society of Literature*

Library records

W*hat do we, as a nation, care about books? How much do you think we spend altogether on out libraries, public or private, as compared with what we spend on our horses?* **John Ruskin**

Every person in the UK pays the equivalent of 26 pence per week towards the public library service. Expenditure on books by public libraries throughout the UK fell by 6.6% last year. Expenditure on books per capita fell by 6.9%. London has lost an average of around 5 libraries a year over the past 10 years.

I pray that no child of mine would ever descend into such a place as a library. They are indeed most dangerous places and unfortunate is she or he who is lured into such a hellhole of enjoyment, stimulus, facts, passion and fun. **Willy Russell**

Children's fiction and non-fiction constitute the largest proportion of book borrowing in the UK, followed by general fiction, adult non-fiction, mystery and detection, and light romance. Goscinny, author of the *Asterix* books, is by far the most loaned foreign author from UK public libraries, being issued over 1,000,000 times in 1991, compared to such names as Molly Keane and Francoise Sagan (over 100,000 times) and well above Albert Camus, Umberto Eco and Sergeanne Gdon (over 40, 000 times). The British Library is Europe's largest national library, with over 18 million books.

Twenty-two acknowledged concubines, and a library of sixty- two thousand volumes attested the variety of his inclinations; and from the productions which he left behind him, it appears that both the one and other were designed for use rather than for ostentation. **Edward Gibbon (on Emperor Gordian the Younger)**

The UK's first 24 hour university library is in Bath. ICI has the largest corporate business library in the UK, while Boots has the largest pharmaceutical library. 54% of public library users borrow books – the remainder borrow audio materials and videos, or use non-borrowing facilities such as reference materials and photocopiers.

Man must not be stifled under paper. Perhaps the various burnings of the Alexandrian Library were necessary, like those Australian Forest Fires without which the new seeds cannot burst their shells and make a young, healthy forest. **William Golding**

Glasgow's Mitchell Library is the largest public library in Europe. Philip Larkin, J Edgar Hoover,

Mao Tse Tung, and Casanova were all librarians. Most borrowed authors (July 1995-June 1996) Estimated loans over one million (4.8% of national loans): Janet and Allan Ahlberg, Dick Francis, Ellis Peters, Enid Blyton, Goscinny, Ruth Rendell, Agatha Christie, Jack Higgins, Danielle Steel, Catherine Cookson, Dick King-Smith, R.L. Stine, Josephine Cox, Ann M. Martin, Kate William, Roald Dahl. Some of the the most borrowed non-fiction titles in the same period: Michael Barrymore *Back in Business;* Jung Chang *Wild Swans: Three Daughters of China;* Rebecca Corfield *Preparing Your Own CV;* Antonia Fraser *The Six Wives of Henry VIII;* Driving Standards Agency *Driving Manual;* Stephen Hawking *A Brief History of Time;* Bob Monkhouse *Crying with Laughter: my Life Story;* Delia Smith *Delia Smith's Winter Collection;* Delia Smith *Delia Smith's Summer Collection;* Christopher Wilson *A Greater Love: Charles and Camilla.* Visiting the library is the fifth most popular pastime in the UK (after visiting a pub, eating in a retaurant, driving for pleasure and eating in a fast food restaurant).

Come, and take choice of all my library, And so beguile thy sorrow. **Titus Andronicus**

A MORI survey for the National Campaign for Learning showed that 49% of adult respondents cited public libraries or museums as their preferred places of learning – significantly more than for schools, colleges or universities. There are 131,033,000 books in the public library service. Last year annual new title acquisitions numbered 4,366, 034 books. Rate paid to authors per loan: 2.07 pence. Percentage of those borrowing at least monthly who are social grade AB 22%, C1 28%, C2 24%, DE 26%. Percentage of heavy book borrowers who read *The News of the World* 22%, *The Sun* 15%, *The Sunday Telegraph* 6%, *The Independent* 5%.

We call ourselves a rich nation, and we are filthy and foolish enough to thumb each other's books out of circulating libraries! **John Ruskin**

In 1998, police confiscated the book *Mapplethorpe* from the library of the University of Central England in Birmingham. Birmingham Central Library subsequently took legal advice and removed a further five of the photographer's books from its shelves. 'Unusual acts of an extreme nature' – police description of the contents of the two photographs (out of the 382 in the book) on which their threatened prosecution was based. 'Wasting police time' – charge which should be brought against the police, according to local MP Jeff Rooker, after borrowing the book through the House of Commons library.

The arsenals of divine vengeance, if I may so describe the Bodleian library. **A.E. Housman**

If a successful libel action results in items being withdrawn by publishers, the Bodleian will withdraw them to a 'Reserved Collection' which is unavailable to readers, but not discard them. Publications which have been known to be banned by prison libraries include *Class War* and *Fight Racism, Fight Imperialism.* British prisons restrict the number of books prisoners can have in their possession using 'volumatic control' – meaning the possessions allowed are restricted by volume. ❏

Statisitics compiled by **Ipsita Mondal**

word power

from *Bookshop Memories*, George Orwell

But our principal sideline was a lending library – the usual 'twopenny no-deposit' library of five or six hundred volumes, all fiction.

Our shop stood exactly on the frontier between Hampstead and Camden Town, and we were frequented by all types from baronets to bus-conductors. Probably our library subscribers were a fair cross-section of London's reading public. It is therefore worth noting that of all the authors in our library the one who 'went out' the best was – Priestley? Hemingway? Walpole? Wodehouse? No, Ethel M. Dell, with Warwick Deeping a good second and Jeffrey Farnol, I should say, third. Dell's novels, of course, are read solely by women, but by women of all kinds and ages and not, as one might expect, merely by wistful spinsters and the fat wives of tobacconists. Roughly speaking, what one might call the average novel – the ordinary, good-bad, Galsworthy-and-water stuff which is the norm of the English novel – seems to exist only for women. Men read either the novels it is possible to respect, or detective stories. But their consumption of detective stories is terrific. One of our subscribers to my knowledge read four or five detective stories every week for over a year, besides others which he got from another library. What chiefly surprised me was that he never read the same book twice. Apparently the whole of that frightful torrent of trash was stored for ever in his memory. He took no notice of titles or author's names, but he could tell by merely glancing into a book whether he had 'had it already'.

In a lending library you see people's real tastes, not their pretended ones, and one thing that strikes you is how completely the 'classical' English novelists have dropped out of favour. It is simply useless to put Dickens, Thackeray, Jane Austen, Trollope, etc into the ordinary lending library; nobody takes them out. At the mere sight of a nineteenth-century novel people say, 'Oh, but that's *old*!' and shy away immediately. Yet it is always fairly easy to *sell* ❑

MARIA MARGARONIS

Purgation and liberation

Enjoy the freedom of a bookless world; purge the libraries and create society anew. People have been burning books, even if only in the imagination, for centuries and for many reasons

'When it was proclaimed that the Library comprised all books, the first impression was one of extravagant joy. All men felt themselves lords of a secret, intact treasure. There was no personal or universal problem whose eloquent solution did not exist – in some hexagon. ... The uncommon hope was followed, naturally enough, by deep depression.'
Jorge Luis Borges, *The Library of Babel*

'The Library is desolation, it has a smell of its own of stagnation and death.'
William Carlos Williams, *Paterson*

'The history of the libraries of antiquity often ends in flames.'
Luciano Canfora, *The Vanished Library*

What passionate reader has not dreamed, at times, of burning all the books? Of being free from the dry, solitary love affair with paper and print, from the knowledge that nine lifetimes could not make a dent in what there is to read, from the suspicion that some natty paperback or portly tome already contains your every living thought? Of going out bookless, naked and unmediated, to meet the world?

The conflagration that supposedly destroyed the library of Alexandria is the first in a long series of real and imaginary fires that punctuate the history of written culture. If classical sources had not given us tantalising hints of a blaze that perhaps consumed a great collection of plays, poetry, philosophy and science, we would have had to invent it. The dream of the lost library allows us to imagine a Holy Grail of ancient wisdom more complete, more mysterious than anything we could have had if all the texts were saved: a Grail not of power but of infinite possibility.

For every real book destroyed in the name of Christianity, Rome, Islam, morality, the Emperor, the Reich, hundreds more have burned in the imagination of writers. Some of those fires parody the bonfires of the censors – the flames that purge Don Quixote's library to cure him of the malaise of chivalry, the heat that burns the texts in the dystopian future of Ray Bradbury's *Fahrenheit 451*. Others, though, are fires of liberation – the fire that destroys the life and work of the obsessive scholar Peter Kien in Canetti's *Auto-da-Fe*, or the one that sweeps the library in Williams's long poem 'Paterson', 'so that nothing that is not green will survive'.

For both censor and creator, the root of this pyromania probably lies in a primitive suspicion of writing as a form of necromancy, a black art of power. A book, like a human being, is mind incomprehensibly contained in matter, the word made flesh. When Bradbury's rebels resist the censors by becoming their best-loved books – memorising their contents, assuming their titles as names – they are reversing the terms of an old, intuitive metaphor that sees the book as vessel for the mind that made it, as a lamp might hold a genie. 'Here, master licentiate,' cries Quixote's housekeeper, rushing out with a bowl of holy water, 'pray take and sprinkle the closet, lest some one of the many enchanters contained in these books, should exercise his art upon us, as a punishment for our burning, and banishing them from the face of the earth.' Burning the books unknots the paradox, freeing the spirit to rise up to heaven, reunited with the air.

Over the centuries, the idea of the book as container for a kind of life has been contested in many battles over knowledge and power. Plato's 'Seventh Letter', an early piece of academic politics, argued that true philosophy cannot be written down: 'Acquaintance with it must come rather after a long period of attendance on instruction ... and close companionship when, suddenly, like a blaze kindled by a leaping spark, it is generated in the soul and at once becomes self-sustaining.' St Paul, that wily neo-Platonist, deployed the same concept in his war of attrition against the people of the Book: 'For the letter killeth, but the spirit giveth life.' Goebbels rang his changes on it at the pyre of some 20,000 volumes in 1933: 'From these ashes will rise the phoenix of the new spirit.'

John Milton, in his great testament to a free press, *Areopagitica,* argued for the letter's capacity to hold the spirit alive – 'For Books are not absolutely dead things, but do contain a potency of life in them to be as active as that soul was whose progeny they are' – but even he hinted that a book has something of the sarcophagus about it: 'A good Book is the precious life-blood of a master spirit, embalmed and treasured up on purpose to a life beyond life.' From there it is a short step to Romanticism's rejection of the bookish Enlightenment (Faust: 'Is it not dust, that fills my hundred shelves/And walls me in like any pedant hack?') and on to Williams's ecstatic, devastating library fire, paradoxical by-product of his modernist's search for living beauty through the world of words: 'Beautiful Thing/the flame's lover...'

Of course, Williams, the good doctor, also sees the library as a bulwark for the bookish against the knowledge of human suffering. The twentieth century, age of literacy, painstakingly traces culture's complicity in violence and oppression as well as liberation: the soul of the book against the soul of man. As early as 1910, EM Forster's Leonard Bast, an aspirant clerk, is killed by a falling bookcase in *Howards' End*. In 1968, after two world wars, Adrienne Rich writes 'The Burning of Paper Instead of Children' in response to a neighbour who complains about her son's burning of a maths textbook: 'The burning of a book,' she says 'arouses terrible sensations in me, memories of Hitler; there are few things that upset me so much as the idea of burning a book.' 'In America we have only the present tense,' counters the writer. 'I am in danger. You are in danger. The burning of a book arouses no sensation in me. I know it hurts to burn. There are flames of napalm in Catonsville, Maryland. I know it hurts to burn. The typewriter is overheated, my mouth is burning, I cannot touch you and this is the oppressor's language.'

Of course, the choice so starkly suggested in Rich's title is a rhetorical extreme; more often the burning of books and the burning of children go together. My imaginary passionate reader, dreaming of freedom and conflagrations, will always wind the film back, unblacken the pages, let the flames retreat into themselves and leave the library intact. But these bookish rebellions against the rule of books are a salutary reminder: a book may harbour a soul, but you can never make a human being out of words. ❏

Maria Margaronis is a contributing editor of The Nation

word power

from *Fahrenheit 451*, Ray Bradbury

'Would you like, some day, Montag, to read Plato's *Republic*?'

'Of course!'

'*I* am Plato's *Republic*. Like to read Marcus Aurelius? Mr Simmons is Marcus.'

'How do you do?' said Mr Simmons.

'Hello,' said Montag.

'I want you to meet Jonathan Swift, the author of that evil political book, *Gulliver's Travels*! And this other fellow is Charles Darwin, and this one is Schopenhauer, and this one is Einstein, and this one here at my elbow is Mr Albert Schweitzer, a very kind philosopher indeed. Here we all are, Montag. Aristophanes and Mahatma Gandhi and Gautama Buddha and Confucius and Thomas Love Peacock and Thomas Jefferson and Mr Lincoln, if you please. We are also Matthew, Mark, Luke and John.'

Everyone laughed quietly.

'It can't *be*,' said Montag.

'It *is*,' replied Granger, smiling. '*We're* book-burners, too. We read the books and burnt them, afraid they'd be found. Micro-filming didn't pay off; we were always travelling, we didn't want to bury the film and come back later. Always the chance of discovery. Better to keep it in the old heads, where no one can see it or suspect it. We are all bits and pieces of history and literature and international law. Byron, Tom Paine, Machiavelli or Christ, it's here. ❏

UNIVERSITY OF CAMBRIDGE

CENSORSHIP
SUMMER SCHOOL

1 – 14 August 1999

Applications are invited for a new interdisciplinary programme which will address aspects of the nature, history and future of censorship worldwide, taking as its theme *the end of Censorship...?*

A major series of plenary lectures will examine areas such as the censorship of journalism, ideas, politics, literature, film, television and cyberspace. These will be complemented by special focus seminars which will allow for close and continuing discussion with speakers and fellow participants.

The Summer School will be valuable for students and faculty in a wide range of subjects from history and literature to political science and communications. It will also provide a forum for the exchange of ideas between professionals and others for whom censorship issues are of significant interest or direct concern.

For further details of this opportunity for intensive study at the University of Cambridge as part of an international community, please contact:

International Division (ref IOC), University of Cambridge Madingley Hall, Madingley, Cambridge, CB3 8AQ, England Tel: +44 (0) 1954 280220. Fax: +44 (0) 1954 280200 Email: rdi1000@cam.ac.uk http://www.cam.ac.uk/CambUniv/ContEd/IntSummer

JASMINA TESANOVIC

Secrets and lies

A library can illuminate the past; it can also trap us in it

My father never said a word about his past. Oh, yes, he would tell stories. And good stories they were, well told. He comes from a part of the world, Herzegovina, where everyone is poor and always was poor; under the Turks, under the Austrians, under the Yugoslavs, under the Bosnians. Or just poor on their own account. They hardly knew how to write, but they knew how to tell tales. And telling tales meant talking about themselves and others, tales full of lies, intentional or otherwise, lively narratives with robust rhythms and rhymes. But my father never really revealed much about himself. Outside the ready-made poetry of his people and his more than average poverty, above average success, there really wasn't much to say.

My mother, on the contrary, kept silent. My mother was a woman with a big secret, besides that of being a mother to me, which was the biggest secret I could imagine existing in the world. Small, stern and silent, not at all like me, it seemed that whatever was said about her wasn't true enough: that words couldn't reveal her tiny, hidden nucleus. Her own inner life was an Invisible, Hidden, Big and maybe Dangerous Secret. Her whole life, and mine too, of course, depended on keeping that secret. After many years of living happily with my mother's secret, a fortune teller told me my mother had a big secret. I asked her not to reveal it to me. One of the things I like best in this harsh, cruel life is that wonderful, invisible but very real space occupied by the aura that surrounds everyone's body. The outer odour and colour of inner intimacy. The space of a secret.

I always thought it must be a love story. Love stories, if they are not secret, can hardly be stories of love, but of children or marriage or divorce. Public stories in any case. And love story it was, my fortune teller said, a big love story which, for some reason or other, had led her

Vivien Leigh as Scarlet O'Hara – Credit Rex/GWTW

out of her home, out of her predestined life as the youngest child of a wealthy southern Serbian family, and into a void, which brought her to my father and eventually me. I used to say Scarlett O'Hara had more influence on my childhood than my mother, but I didn't realise at the time the significance of what I was saying: my mother *was* Scarlett

O'Hara. Not only did she look like her, the south of Serbia with its fascist aristocracy has much in common with the southern states of the new continent, being new, rich and primitive; both conservative and heroic in its lack of authentic tradition. Now, Scarlett O'Hara was a substitute for the mother whose secret prevented me from dealing openly with her .

So my father told lies and my mother had secrets; while my mother hated lies and my father despised secrets. A perfect marriage, symbiotic, with hardly any space for a child or truth.

As a very small child in desperate search of truth, I found it in books: books of all kinds, fairy tales, mysteries, philosophy, history, fiction. I truly believed that all the patrimony and wisdom of this world lay in books. And of course The Truth. Whenever I had a problem, a question, I would look it up in some book. But my parents very quickly noticed this sickness in their only child: I wouldn't go out and play with children, but read books; I wouldn't study science but read stories; I wouldn't speak straight but as in books. I even invented my own words instead of repeating those they taught me at school. They thought it was all my granny's fault. Every night she would tell me a new and true story: about mermaids who became women and changed the world, about salt mills at the bottom of the sea that made the sea rich and salty, about children who knew better then their parents but couldn't change the world. She tried to explain the unexplainable, to soothe the daily pain of not understanding, of being excluded, through stories. So they banned books from the house. They said books were idling, books were dusty and books were expensive. They wanted me to study a trade, live in a nice clean barren room and buy myself a brand new dress. It was the sixties, it was the potent, technocrat, communist, winning generation of parents from the East living in the West and making the most of it. They were, however, afraid of both, East and West, which might corrupt their ideal project, their only child: Me.

I remember a story my parents used to tell me about the first years of their marriage. My father would lift my mother onto the top of a cupboard with her books, so that she could study without distractions. By distractions he meant music, other people, cooking and cleaning. She couldn't climb down, being too small and without the will to defy his decision that she should finish university in time.

I remember it as a terrible story for which I could find no decent explanation. Why study on the top of an uncomfortable cupboard, set apart from the people and things we love? Again books. An Unavoidable Devil, but Devil nonetheless. When I think of my mother in that context, I think of her as a victim, a victim of books and of my father at the same time, someone who cannot live with pleasure, whose principle of Enlightment and Joy has been cut down by the stern role of Science and Men. I would feel sorry for her then, as I do now, but she never did. She would tell me: 'That is my choice too. One shouldn't fool around with books or men.'

My parents were both communists. For my father, becoming a communist during the war against Nazis and fascists was a matter of life and death; for my mother it was a free choice, a choice against a free life. In her native town before the war, communists were persecuted, tortured and killed as terrorists. She was 17 and she was an idealist. And I know more: she was against her patriarchal family of Big Brothers who jealously controlled her privacy and chastity. She had no space for a normal, everyday life of fun and joy. She had to be a saint. With her explosive temperament, she could only stay alive by becoming an idealist.

In 1948, when Stalin was declared a traitor to Yugoslavia, she refused to follow the orders of her party. She refused to believe in concentration camps, in gulags, in the terrors of the Soviet Union. Then and now, with emotion but without explanations.

My father, however, denounced Stalin, then Tito, then the entire ideology that had saved his life. She didn't. Then, as now, she is ready to risk her and my life for the idea of communism.

As I said, my mother is a woman with a secret, one big secret and many small ones. She thinks secretly and reads books secretly. Once upon a time, she told me only recently, she had a big library. It was a family treasure; some members of the family used it, others didn't. She did. When she was not playing with her puppy, she idled and dreamed with her books in her library. Her dog waited outside. Then, one day, she became a communist, and communism taught her that idling and dreaming took her to an unjust world of arts and lies while people were dying of hunger and pain without her help. She decided to do something about it: she took all her books outside and made a huge bonfire: her kulak father's library burned. She left home, never again spoke to two of her three brothers who were anti-communists, married my father, a poor self-made engineer, never took a penny from her inheritance and never told me about her life before she became a communist. She tells of a friend of hers from a similar background, who burned her library together with her family house: she didn't even bother to take the books out.

When I'm not reading books I write them. In all my books I speak of my mother, with passion. The first time she read my story about her she said: 'But these are all lies. You, too, write lies in books then? Is that why you became a writer, to become a liar?'

I told her not to read my next book: 'It's all lies again,' I said. But she answered sternly and bravely: 'You are my daughter, you are a writer and I am proud of you. When somebody asks me, is it true what your daughter says in her books, I will say my daughter is a writer and she is free to write as she pleases.'

My mother, as I said, had a secret: she never wrote books, she burned her own library, she gave away her things, her tradition, her money to her ideals, to a better future she believed in and still believes in. And I am only a writer. Somewhere in between, maybe in those burned books, lies her secret. Maybe it wasn't a love story after all, or maybe it was love letters she was burning with her library. It is I now whose turn it is to find out what was in those mysterious books which deserved to burn. By writing them, or living them? Who knows which is the shortcut to wisdom? Wisdom is a privilege of old age but only those who weren't wise and rational in youth acquire it, says Hannah Arendt.

Of one thing I am certain: she will never tell me her secret outright because she burned her library and because I write fantasies and lies. I am unable to unveil her secret, to reach out for that mysterious book of Truth my mother burned on that hot summer day many years before I was born, leaving behind her just the barren soil of her Tara, sacked first by Nazi occupiers then by Russian 'liberators' and finally by the local New Order. But she sent me a clear message: 'Never Look Back, Tomorrow is Another Day.' ❏

Jasmina Tesanovic is a freelance writer and feminist publisher (Publisher 94) from Belgrade. Publications include In Exile *(94),* Women Stories *(95),* Mermaids, *(97),* On Normality: a Moral Opera of a Political Idiot *(to be published in 1999).*

word power

from *The Handmaid's Tale*, Margaret
Atwood

My presence here is illegal. It is forbidden for us to be alone with the Commanders. We are for breeding purposes: we aren't concubines, geisha girls, courtesans. On the contrary: everything possible has been done to remove us from that category. There is supposed to be nothing entertaining about us, no room is to be permitted for the flowering of secret lusts; no special favours are to be wheedled, by them or us, there are to be no toeholds for love. We are two-legged wombs; that's all: sacred vessels, ambulatory chalices.

So why does he want to see me, at night, alone?

If I'm caught, it's to Serena's tender mercies I'll be delivered. he isn't supposed to meddle in such household discipline, that's women's business. After that, reclassification. I could become an Unwoman.

But to refuse to see him could be worse. There's no doubt about who holds the real power.

But there must be something he wants, from me. To want is to have a weakness. It's this weakness, whatever it is, that entices me. It's like a small crack, in a wall, before now impenetrable. If I press my eye to it, this weakness of his, I may be able to see my way clear.

I want to know what he wants.

I raise my hand, knock, on the door of this forbidden room where I have never been, where women do not go. Not even Serena Joy comes here, and the cleaning is done by Guardians. What secrets, what male totems are kept in here?

I'm told to enter. I open the door, step in.

What is on the other side is normal life. I should say: what is on the other side looks like normal life. There is a desk, of course, with a Computalk on it, and a black leather chair behind it. There's a potted plant on the desk, a pen-holder set, papers. There's an oriental rug on the floor, and a fireplace without a fire in it. There's a small sofa, covered in brown plush, a television set, an end table, a couple of chairs.

But all around the walls there are bookcases. They're filled with books. Books and books and books, right out in plain view, no locks, no boxes. No wonder we can't come in here. It's an oasis of the forbidden. I try not to stare. ❑

DORIS LESSING

Books for the hungry

Even in the simplest surroundings, books and the learning they bring are the staff of life

It is an astonishing fact that Zimbabwe, after 20 years of a rule that has starved libraries and schools of books, is full of people who yearn for books, who see them as a key to a better life, and whose attitude is similar to that of people in Europe and the USA up to 50 years ago who read because they agreed with Carlyle's dictum 'the real education is a good library' – and aspired to be educated.

There are libraries and libraries. Some I am involved with would not be recognised as such in more fortunate parts of the world. A certain trust sends boxes of books out to villages which might seem to the ill-informed no more than clusters of poor thatched mud huts, but in them may be retired teachers, teachers on holiday, people with three or four years of education who yearn for better. These villages may have no electricity, telephone, running water, but they beg for books from every visitor. Perhaps a hut may be set aside for books, with a couple of shelves in it, or shelves or a trestle may be put under a tree. In a bush village far from any big town, or even a little one, such a trestle with 40 books on it has transformed the life of the area. Instantly study groups appeared, literacy classes – people who can read teaching those who can't – civic classes and groups of aspirant writers. A letter from there reads: 'People cannot live without water. Books are our water and we drink from this spring.'

An enterprising council official in Bulawayo sends out books by donkey car – 'our travelling library' – to places where ordinary transport cannot go, because there are no roads, or roads that succumb to dust or mud.

A friend of mine, known to be involved with organisations that supply books, was approached by two youths in a bush village near Lake Kariba who said, 'We have built a library, now please give us the books.' The library was a shelf in a little lean-to of grass and poles, but the books would never succumb to white ants or the book-devouring fish-moth, because they would always be out on loan.

A survey was made in the villages and it turned out that what these book-starved people yearn for are romances, detective stories, poetry, adventures, biography, novels of all kinds, short stories. Exactly what a survey in this country would reveal – that is, among people who still read.

One problem is that these people do not know what is available that they might like if they tried. *The Mayor of Casterbridge* was a school set book one year and was read by the adults, and so people ask for books by Hardy.

The most popular book everywhere is George Orwell's *Animal Farm*. Another that has queues waiting for it is *World Tales* by Idries Shah, and it is not only the tales themselves, but the scholarly footnotes attached to them which people enjoy. They say of a story, perhaps from the Sudan or the USA, 'But we have a story just like that.'

One problem is that people, hearing of this book hunger, at once offer to donate their cast-off books. These are not always suitable. Donations would be better. Book Aid International, based in London, sends books out to book-starved countries. ❏

Doris Lessing's latest novel is Mara and Dann *(HarperCollins, 1999). Book Aid International can be reached at 39 Coldharbour Lane, London, SE5. Tel (44) 171 733 3577*

ANON

The adventures of Mr X

'There's no better friend than a book.' 'A book is a kind companion.' 'A book is the enemy of loneliness.' 'A book is a ray of light in the darkness.' And so on and so forth. Although these were no more than slogans to the authorities, as far as Mr X was concerned they were the essence of truth.

He had trod the pavement along *Enqelab* (Revolution) Avenue thousands of times. Most of the booksellers knew him by now. He was enraptured by books. One hundred pages of a novel at lunchtime, 20 pages of poetry by way of an afternoon snack, 10 couplets by Shams or Hafez as an appetiser and 40 pages of another book for supper. He had poor eyesight and wore thick, pebble glasses that had left a permanent mark on the bridge of his nose. His greatest passion was to stand behind shop windows and gobble up the books!

Mr X was on first name terms with many of the second-hand booksellers along the Avenue. He would often buy second-hand books, read them carefully, then return them as part exchange for another book. He considered this an excellent arrangement.

In his workplace, too, everyone knew he was a bookworm. Instead of attending to the clients or carrying out the boss's orders, he would secretly read books.

Underneath his desk, he had set up what was, to all intents and purposes, a library.

In the course of his frequent visits to the bookshops, Mr X occasionally witnessed some strange going-ons. Once, for example, when he was buying the full, bound volumes of Dr Safa's *History of Literature*, he saw a smartly dressed couple, obviously from the best part of town, ordering a hardback, gold-embossed, large format edition of a book. The shop owner said, 'We don't have it, but we'll order it for you.' Then, to his even greater amazement, Mr X saw the man take out a cheque made out for an astronomical sum and, after signing it with a flourish, hand it to the shop owner.

And it has to be said that, although there are many people in society who, for lack of money or unfamiliarity with books, never have anything to do with them, there are others who purchase them by the metre to furnish their bookshelves. Not to mince words, the book snobs outnumber the bookworms.

Mr X had tramped the pavement along *Enqelab* Avenue thousands of times. It was considered the best place to go if you were looking for books. On the far side of the square, in the basement of a house, you could buy all kinds of books printed 30 years ago or more for 100 *tomans* each. That was the place he loved above all others. He would buy books that were falling to pieces and stick them back together at home using sellotape and glue and bits of cloth. Then he would lovingly read them one by one.

In the beginning, he didn't really give a thought to where all these books had come from but, of late, Mr X has begun to wise up a bit and his curiosity is aroused: he wants to find out what on earth is going on.

The first second-hand bookseller, who always set up his stall in front of the bank, had said: 'I swear to you we buy good, rare books from individuals and private libraries.' A second bookseller, who sat a little further down, opposite the eastern depot's bus stop, had laughed and said: 'Mr X, these are all photocopies. What I'm trying to say is, some people photocopy the books and bring them to us.'

But Mr X said: 'If these books are photocopies and not real prints, why is there so much white space bordering the pages?'

And the bookseller had replied: 'Well, lots of them are second-hand books.'

But Mr X, with his inborn intelligence, had persisted: 'If they're second-hand, why do they look so new?'

'Mr X, why trouble yourself with such things, just buy your books!'

He had climbed up the stairs. In a room measuring three by four, thousands of old books are piled up one on top of the other. Some newly-published books, such as Dante's *Divine Comedy, Aisha after the Prophet, Dear Uncle Napoleon*, Patience Stone, were stacked in a corner.

The attendant had said only that these books were brought to Tehran from Isfahan, Tabriz and Mashhad. Nothing more was forthcoming..

Now, it occurs to Mr X that the distribution network for these rare or banned books consists of a vast Mafia. But, as far as Mr X is concerned, there isn't a mystery alive that can't be solved. All he has to do is investigate like an undercover detective to get to the bottom of things.

★★★★★

We've already said that Mr X beat a constant path along *Enqelab* Avenue. Now he also kept asking himself this question: how can it be that a book published in an edition of 3,000 many years ago is still available, in mint condition and selling at a high price, at every bookshop and second-hand book stall?

One of the distributors of old books, who had decided to go down the path of honesty, told Mr X: 'These books aren't published in either Isfahan or Tabriz. It's not even a question of secret, underground publishers. These books are published by large, well-known publishers who obtained publication permits for the books many years ago. They are published without obtaining [new, post-revolution] permits, either without the required registration details or using the registration details of the old editions. On the inside cover of any book, you'll find the book's registration details, such as the title of the book, the number of copies printed, the publisher's name and so on. This same edition is reprinted 60 times and, if you ask me, it isn't the publishers' fault. The blame lies with the Guidance Ministry which refuses to issue permits for new editions despite the demand from readers!!'

When Mr X had asked about the way these books were distributed, he'd been told: 'We usually give these books to bookshops without invoices or using fake invoices, using the titles of other books.' He'd also heard that much the same thing applied to the printing of posters in Iran!

And a publisher, who told Mr X never to reveal his name, had confided: 'The publishing, printing and selling of books takes place within a vast Mafia network. We even have distributors who barely know how to read and write, but they've ordered books from us in their own name. Books are a commodity and sell at amazing and unpredictable prices. Given the presence of these illiterate dealers, the book market has taken on a bizarre form and shape.'

The black market in books has thousands of peculiarities that would amaze the listener.

As he trod his pavement along *Enqelab* Avenue, past the university one last time, Mr X ran his eyes over the large number of book dealers, black market books and bookshops, and felt as if he was walking along a ribbon enveloped in night. And he kept muttering these phrases under his breath: 'There's no better friend than a book. A book is a kind companion. A book is the enemy of loneliness. A book is a ray of light in the darkness...' ❑

'The adventures of Mr X on the book black market' appeared in the Tehran daily Akhbar *(News) in November 1998 during Iran's Book Week*

Translated by Nilou Mobasser

Embattled books

Last year alone, 478 challenges – attempts to remove materials from public libraries, schools and school libraries – were reported to the American Library Association

The American Library Association estimates that for every challenge against books reported, four to five go unreported.

The number of challenges reported rose in the early part of this decade, from 157 reported in 1990 to 762 in 1995. An overwhelming majority of challenges are made by parents, who made 3096 reported complaints during the 1990's. Most of the books were challenged on the basis of being too sexually explicit, (1299 challenges last year) followed by challenges for 'offensive language' (1134), for being 'unsuited to age group' (1062), for mentioning things to do with Satan and the Occult (744), violence (562), and homosexuality (474). Below is a list of the ten most frequently challenged books in 1998.

#1 MOST CHALLENGED FICTION: *The Chocolate War* by Robert Cormier – accused of being sexually explicit, offensive and innappropriate to age group

#1 MOST CHALLENGED NON-FICTION: *It's Perfectly Normal* by Robie Harris – accused of being too sexually explicit for children

ALSO CHALLENGED:

Of Mice and Men by John Steinbeck (offensive language; unsuited to age group)

Goosebumps and *Fear Street* series by R. L. Stine (depicting occult and satanic themes)
I Know Why the Caged Bird Sings by Maya Angelou (too explicit in its portrayal of rape)

The Giver by Lois Lowry (offensive language; focus on death)

Always Running by Luis Rodriguez (for being violent, racist and unsuited to teenagers)

Crazy Lady by Jane Leslie Conly (offensive language)

Blubber by Judy Blume (offensive language; innapropriate for age group)

Source: ALA Office of Intellectual Freedom, 50 East Huron Street, Chicago, Illinois 60611-2795; email:oif@ala.org; http://www.ala.org/oif.html ❏

Statistics compiled by **Emily Mitchell**

Lost libraries of the 20th century

1914 *Belgium* Following the German invasion of Belgium at the beginning of World War I, German soldiers set fire to the library of the Catholic University of Louvain on August 25.

1932 *Spain* A fire severely damaged the University of Valencia library during the Spanish Civil War.

1933, 1935 *Germany* After the Nazi seizure of power, a number of public library officials prepared black lists of prohibited authors, amounting to about 10 per cent of public library collections. These also paved the way for the public burning of books on 10 May, 1933. A further list of 5,500 prohibited books was prepared in 1935. Many of these books were destroyed.

1937-1945 *China* During the Sino-Japanese War, a great many private and public libraries were destroyed. These included the libraries at:
National University of Tsing Hua, Peking; University Nan-k'ai, T'ien-chin; Institute of Technology of He-pei, T'ien-chin; Medical College of He-pei, Pao-ting; Agricultural College of He-pei, Pao-ting; University Ta Hsia, Shang-hai; University Kuang Hua, Shang-hai; National University of Hu-nan; University of Nanking; Royal Asiatic Society, Shanghai; University of Shanghai; Soochow University.

1938-1945:
Czechoslovakia Soon after the German takeover of the Sudetenland, all Czech books in libraries in this territory dealing with geography, biography and history were confiscated, together with the works of many Czech writers.

Poland The Germans embarked upon a policy of ruthless destruction of Polish libraries, archives and museums. These included: the Raczynski Library and the Science Society Library, in Poznan; the Cathedral Library; the National Library in Warsaw; the Central Military Library. The Germans formed 'Brenn-Kommandos' (arson-squads) to destroy Jewish synagogues and books. Thus the Great Talmudic Library of the Jewish Theological Seminary in Lublin was burned. On the eve of the German evacuation of Poland in January 1945, the main stacks of the Warsaw Public Library were burned.

Germany It has been estimated that a third of all German books were destroyed during World War II. The greatest losses occurred at libraries in: Aachen, Berlin, Bonn, Bremen, Carmstadt, Dortmund, Dresden, Essen, Frankfurt, Giessen, Greifswald, Hamburg, Hannover, Karlsruhe, Kassel, Kiel, Leipzig, Magdeburg, Marburg, Munchen, Munster, Nurnberg, Stuttgart, Wurzburg,

Baltic States After the occupation by Soviet troops an official list of Banned Books and Brochures was issued in Latvia in November 1940. With additional lists, over 4,000 titles were proscribed. In Latvia, as in Estonia and Lithuania, such books were removed from bookstores and libraries and, in many cases, publicly burned.

France During the German Occupation many libraries were destroyed, or had their books confiscated and replaced with German books. The greatest losses occurred

in: Alsace-Lorraine, Beauvais, Caen, Chartres, Dieppe, Douai, Le Havre, Metz, Paris, Strasbourg, Tours.
Belgium Library of the Catholic University of Louvain and the Public Library of Tournay were both destroyed by shelling.
The Netherlands The Provincial Library of Zeeland was destroyed by bombs.
Italy Italian libraries suffered damage as a result of Allied and German air raids. More than 20 municipal libraries were destroyed and many public libraries suffered the same fate. Some of the worst hit cities were Milan, Naples, Parma and Turin.
United Kingdom Libraries were damaged by bombs in Bristol, Coventry, Liverpool and London
Serbia The National Library in Belgrade was completely destroyed by German bombs.
Soviet Union Heavy damage was done to Russian libraries. It has been estimated that more than 100 million books were destroyed, mainly from public libraries.
Japan Air raids did heavy damage to libraries and collections, including the Cabinet Library in Tokyo.
Austria About 100 manuscripts and 4,500 volumes of academic publications were lost from the University Library of Graz as a result of plunder.
Hungary Nearly all small libraries were destroyed and many of the larger libraries suffered serious damage during the siege of Budapest.
Romania About 300,000 volumes from public libraries were destroyed as a result of the war.

1946 *Germany,* A collection of about 270,000 (out of 400,000) volumes was confiscated by the Russian authorities from the *Thüringische Landesbücherei,* Gotha and removed to the Soviet Union. These included manuscripts and incunabulas.

1947 *Pakistan* As a result of communal riots, two of the largest libraries of the

Indian subcontinent in Lahore were damaged.

1949-1957 *China* Following the communist takeover, libraries all over the country were purged of 'reactionary, obscene and absurd' publications.

1966-1976 *China* During the Cultural Revolution, a systematic effort was made to purge and destroy all 'politically incorrect books'. All libraries were closed for various lengths of time between 1966 and 1970. Some were closed permanently and burned. Others were thoroughly purged, only the books of Marx, Lenin and Mao being spared. Although no record has been kept of the losses, it is clear that destruction of books took place on an unprecedented scale.

1966 *Tibet* In 1966, the Cultural Revolution wrought havoc in this Chinese-occupied country too. Red Guards invaded the leading monastery in Tibet and destroyed frescoes and irreplaceable historic manuscripts.

1976-1979 *Cambodia* Following their rise to power, the Khmer Rouge systematically began to destroy all vestiges of 'corrupt' culture. In the National Library in Phnom Penh, the Khmer Rouge threw out and burned most of the books and all bibliographical records; less than 20 percent of the collection survived.

This list was taken from: *Memory of the World: Lost Memory – Libraries and Archives destroyed in the Twentieth Century,* UNESCO, Paris, 1996. It can be viewed on the web at: *www.unesco.org/webworld/mdm/administ/en/d etruit.html*

YANG LIAN

The sea stands still

Brecht's Last Question

winter signifying blackening pine trees
snow   signifying in an unoccupied room
lamplight from morning to night

lighting up   an occupied graveyard
a disrobed skull makes you more like a poet
taking off outside the window the public role of your last life

signifying a visit to your own frozen smile
the binding of glass   the contents a snowstorm
death's repertoire   a menu of the city

let the bell's song between both your endpoints be handclaps
two of you   imagining each other
ugly birds of hands writing the phoney grey sky

it signifies the dead have long ago seen
this headstone outside the study window   like a letter of condolence
the green of every pine needle finally rented out

let the antagonistic   the extant
the whole flawless twilight invent your madness
ask   what has night got
night has died twice   what can it still hope for

Butterfly of Revenge

The butterfly you poisoned had a human face
gloomy jet-black wings   are bound to have memory
remember   the feminine madness of its last dive toward you

hatred   thinks itself a flower
in the misconceptions of bright morning
a black powder-puff   puffs the gaudy room full of nightmare
again the butterfly waits on the wall you fear to see

shredded by your hand   it finds you
turned to shadow   shockingly surrounded by the wind's voice
a tiny mouth that bites you   after death

it's bound to belong to someone   invading the green sky backwards
the more you want to forget
the more you see the butterfly is taking its revenge

Yang Lian *is a Chinese poet living in exile in London. Poems from* Where the sea stands still, *a bilingual edition, translations by Brian Bolton (Bloodaxe Books)*

EMILY MITCHELL

The joys of literacy

Twenty-three per cent of adults in the UK have poor literacy: six per cent can barely read at all

Once we've mastered it, reading becomes a skill that we take for granted. We forget the years of struggling to memorise characters and words, and rules that are always more broken than observed. But for those who learn to read late, the task is fraught with difficulties both practical and emotional. What is it like to be an adult living in a society saturated with written language, and to be unable to read? What is it like finally to learn? I asked a group of literacy students in north London about their experiences. What follows is an edited transcript of conversations with two groups of students (some names have been changed).

One of the students began by talking about her experience of working in a shop...

Soeuad: I thought, I can't say I don't know how to read, because then [the owner] wouldn't let me have the job. He said, when someone comes and asks you for help, you must help them, not tell them you don't know... The first thing I remember, a customer came in and wanted a tin of beans, and I couldn't say 'I don't know where they are' so I'm looking around, thinking 'where is it, where is it,' and the owner picks up a tin from the one of the shelves. So all that day I'm trying to remember the first letter: 'B, B, B, B', for each item, up to that evening... this was a couple of years ago, a long time back when I was about 16, still part time. And all that time, that was the only place where I learned to read.

EM: So you really learned letter by letter?

Souead: That's right. And same with the rest of the things in the shop. He'd say 'tomato juice' and I'd wait till he picked it up, and then he'd go to the customers 'this is it', and I have to try and remember it. He did not know, well, him and his wife did not know.

EM: What about school?

Soueuad: We came here in 1977 from Morocco, with no word of English, so the time that I was going to school, I was learning a bit of the language. Reading and writing are supposed to come after, but I didn't get a chance. The English got easier, but the writing and the spelling didn't. That's why I had to come back after all these years to try. Reading is not much of a problem, its just my spelling that's bad. I had to find a way just to get the reading. It's just because of working in the shop that I could read a few things. I found it helpful, because you've got the item there and the writing on it so you just repeat it. [The shop's owner] never even knew.

EM: What made you decide to take this class?

Angela: For years you just are in frustration because you can't write. I could think of the most beautiful words but I couldn't write them. It's like not having legs and wanting to walk. I can speak and I've got a mind, I may be dyslexic but I thought, lets go and see what I can do about it.

Anna: I was born over here in Britain. Then we moved away and my father wouldn't let me go to school. That's why I've come back now. It's just difficult to get a job. You feel embarrassed when you have to fill in application forms.

Soeuad: Most things have application forms. They say 'send an essay' and stuff like this, and if you are unable to do it, you've got no chance.

AM: And it's not like you don't know the answers, because you do...

Soeuad: You're scared that you are going to do something wrong, that you can't come back and change it. What we learned here is that we do actually know [the answers] already.

EM: Is there anything that you've read in class that you found particularly helpful?

Anna: There was one book we read. Anne Frank. I read it last year and I just can't give it back. I keep meaning to bring it to class, I've got it in my bag now, but I can't bring myself to give it back.

Angela: It's because you can relate to her. Being trapped, outside of everything that's going on around her.

EM: What about writing in class? Is that helpful?

Angela: Yesterday, we had a piece of writing that you'd done (turns to

Anna). She'd written a piece about her school days and about bullying, and she'd had a few spelling mistakes in there. So (the teacher) printed it all up and we all read it and then corrected her spelling mistakes and punctuation and made the sentences shorter. We're learning from each other all the time.

Anna: The more you write at home as well, the more familiar you get with the language because when you can't read and write, you just lose your confidence.

Soeuad: You don't want anyone to mention about writing and reading stuff. And you're always praying no one asks you to fill this or that in.

Angela: Well with me, because my spoken English is so good, people assume that I'm at university and they ask me what I'm studying and whether I'm at university, and I say 'no'. Or 'what job do you do?' They think I've got a high-paid job, because of my spoken English.

Anna: With me, I'm embarrassed to say what I'm studying.

Soeuad: I was waiting at the bus stop just today, talking to someone and they asked 'oh, what do you study?' And I said, 'we just learned the apostrophe.' And I don't get embarrassed about it anymore because you know yourself that you're in the class, you're not sitting at home, you're trying to improve yourself. I'm not ashamed any more to say 'yeah, I'm learning where to put the stops, the apostrophes, how to make a sentence'. Not like before.

Angela: In the schools, there is still... I mean now it's money, before it was status, middle class, working class and upper class. If you came from a middle class family, you probably had someone that did read with you. I didn't have anyone to read with me... I was one of the ones that just slipped through the net. I had some very strange teachers who didn't like black children. You were in the class, but you weren't actually IN the class. They'd give me the work, and I couldn't read anyway, so I wouldn't know what it said. I kind of slipped through all the way up until secondary school.

EM: How would you change the schools that you went to?

Anna: Teachers paying more attention. There's no point in you sitting in the class if you can't do the work. You're sitting out there learning nothing. They should pay more attention and help their students.

Angela: I can put more to that. I think that in the class the teacher will know who's got which strengths and which weaknesses. If she had more time, because they are pushed for time now – I've got children – I find that the teachers are pushed for time. They've got to teach a topic in so many days, and then move on to the next one. They might need more time to get the subject across to some of the children. I think they should have a helper or something. More adults to fewer children. More one to one.

Anna: My teacher used to call me stupid little Greek girl and everyone in the class would hear it. Everyone used to say it to me... It was only me and this Turkish girl, we were best friends, me and her had this licence to do nothing. Always spotted out.

Soeuad: Did you have a word with anybody about the teacher's racist comments?

Anna: You can't, no you can't.

Angela: Because she's the teacher and you are the student.

EM: Do you feel that reading stories by other adult literacy students is valuable?

Angela: Definitely. You feel isolated, don't you? And when you read something like that, you identify, you know there's somebody else who has the same problems.

EM: Have any of you submitted writing to the college magazine? Do you think it is valuable for students to publish their own work?

Anna: Seeing your work printed as well is very important.

Angela: It's a bonus.

Anna: I said to my boyfriend that I was doing work for the college magazine and he started taking the mickey out of me. I said, at least I'm doing something. All my life I wanted to write something to be published. Now's my time.

The second group of students I spoke to were enrolled in a creative writing class. Several of them had previously been enrolled in literacy classes.

Chico: I think the stigma [of having dyslexia] really affected me because I wrote on and off all my life, but I definitely still have hang-ups about not having good English even though I have a degree. It was a stigma of the teaching profession... that they didn't actually realize that these problems were happening in children. Overall everyone was saying that the British education system was so good, look at how many children are coming through it, how many children are literate, when in fact what was happening was a lot of children were coming through it and getting very badly damaged, getting completely ignored and not being literate at all.

Cecil: In my day, if you found out you were thick, the only way you found out you weren't was to go to work. I ended up as a foreman in an engineering firm. Still couldn't spell. So if I had to explain anything, I'd have a couple of friends with me, tell them what I wanted done, get them to write it down, and then read it back to me.

Barbara: When I was in school, we were just left basically: either you learned or you didn't. I spent more time out of school than in it. It wasn't that I didn't want to learn 'cause I did. I taught myself. I got to secondary school and I spent as little time as possible there. I stayed for about four days and that was it. And from then on it was just a case of going to lots of open schools, special schools. I used to go home and do lots of reading and I've always been writing since I can remember.

Chico: I remember once I studied all week for a spelling test and I thought it was going to be impossible. I studied the words all week and went over them and over them. I got nine out of ten for the spelling test and the teacher pulled me aside and said 'I think you were cheating'. When I look back on education, I think what people didn't realise was that teachers affected pupils so much. If you treat a child really badly in primary school then it won't show until later, in secondary and by then the damage is already done. ❏

EM

ARTHUR C CLARKE

Orbital libraries

Nearly 40 years ago, Arthur Clarke foresaw a massive, technology-driven social restructuring. The world we now live in bears out many of his predictions

This note is being written in a tiny fishing village on the south coast of Ceylon, only a few hundred miles from the equator. There are no telephones, no electric light, no newspapers, no cinemas; there are a few battery-powered radios, but reception is poor on the short-waves and impossible on the broadcast band.

It is difficult for a visitor from one of the more developed countries to imagine the social isolation of such a community – though this village is positively suburban when compared with thousands in the more remote parts of Asia and Africa. Most of the human race exists in a cultural vacuum; it is still divided into myriads of insulated villages or tribes, as it has been since the dawn of history. But now, in a brief moment of time, all this will end. The coming of the communications satellite will make it impossible for any human group – indeed, any individual – to be more than a few milliseconds from any other. The social consequences of this, for good or evil, may be as great as those brought about by the printing press or the internal combustion engine. And they will come upon us much more swiftly.

Because they share many common interests (including language), already possess extensive rebroadcasting facilities and are separated by a relatively small time differential, the Americas and western Europe will obviously be the first to benefit from communications satellites. Some of the services which may reasonably be expected, either experimentally or on a full operational basis, during the next decade are:

1. *The Orbital Post Office.* It has been pointed out by S. Metzger that a single 5 mc/s satellite has enough information-handling capacity to carry *all* first-class and air-mail correspondence between the United States and

Europe. Delivery time would be reduced to approximately a half, the limit being set by the physical collection and distribution of the mail. One of the chief problems involved in this system is psychological; how would the public react to a postal service in which its letters could be read by unauthorised persons at any point? However, it accepted wartime V-Mail; and for really confidential correspondence, there would be no difficulty in developing private electronic coding systems, so that only the right recipient could receive readable copy.

As ground facilities improve, to keep up with the possibilities offered by the satellites, we may expect high-speed facsimile systems to spread to at least all important towns. For business (as opposed to personal) needs, the distinction between mail, telegram and teletype will rapidly blur. In each case, transmission time will approach zero, with profound effects upon industry and public affairs, and a speeding up of the tempo of life.

2. *Orbital Newspapers.* The simultaneous setting of international editions has already been demonstrated. Influential newspapers – such as the London and the New York *Times* will experience a great increase in distribution and immediacy. One of the first countries to benefit from this will be, rather ironically, the United States, which has never possessed a really national newspaper. In the longer run, however, the newspaper as we have known it for the last three hundred years cannot be expected to survive the advent of communications satellites; ultimately, the home presentation will become purely electronic.

3. *Intercontinental Telephony.* As more and more bandwidths are made available, there will be a tremendous increase in long-distance telephony. It is impossible to set a limit to this; man is a talkative animal, and all estimates that have been made of his need for communication have been swiftly surpassed.

The full consequences of swift, cheap, and universal person-to-person telephony (and later television) cannot possibly be anticipated at this stage. One can only hint at some trends which may become apparent during the next decade, and dominant during the one that follows. They are: (a) A great decline in personal correspondence, continuing the trend already started by the telephone.

(b) A correspondingly great increase in long-distance personal contacts. The situation will develop over the whole world that now exists in great cities, when intimate friends may talk to each other every day but seldom meet.

(c) A steep decline in transportation for other than pleasure purposes. Efficient communications and efficient transportation are, to some extent, opposing influences. If either were perfect (ie, free and instantaneous) there would be no need for the other. Thus one can envisage the time, in the not-too-distant future, when conferences could be conducted with none of the participants leaving their own countries – or even their own homes.

Now let us look a little further ahead, to the second phase in the development of communications satellites – particularly the impact of direct broadcasting on the undeveloped countries. This, coupled with the timely invention of the transistor, may give a great stimulus to radio; though we usually associate satellites with television, it must not be forgotten that most areas of this planet cannot yet receive reliable, good quality sound.

However, radio brings us immediately to the question of language. A single orbital transmitter can broadcast high-fidelity sound to half the world – but can it provide programmes of equal interest to the Congo Pygmy, the Afghan tribesman, the Greenland Eskimo, the man-about-Manhattan? Obviously not, until they share a common language and, at least to some extent, a common culture.

Communications satellites will make a basic world language mandatory. Just as all men had to learn to read so that they could work and even survive in modern society, so in the one world of the very near future they will have to possess a language in common. There can be little doubt that this language will be English (perhaps Basic English). This has long since ceased to be the property of the English and is now the property of the world – so it can be accepted without reservation even by the newest and most hypersensitive of ex-colonial nations.

The full potentiality of educational programmes from satellites could not be exploited, however, until the arrival of vision; one could hardly teach the written language without this aid. And here I would like to make a suggestion for an interesting compromise between radio and TV.

It should be possible to develop a cheap and simple slow-scan facsimile-plus-sound receiver which could operate on the normal radio bandwidth, without requiring the approximately thousandfold greater spectrum space needed by TV. Such a device could reproduce line drawings and cartoons (halftones would be unnecessary) at a perfectly adequate speed for educational purposes, where the same picture has to stay in view for a minute or more. It would be the remote equivalent of the teacher's blackboard, and with its aid, even language could be taught to peoples who did not share a single word of their instructor's tongue.

The existence of direct-broadcasting TV satellites will immediately focus attention upon two problems which today are merely a minor annoyance, but which tomorrow will be intolerable. They are censorship and jamming. For the advent of communications satellites will mean the end of the present barriers to the free flow of information; no dictatorship can build a wall high enough to stop its citizens listening to the voices from the stars. It would be extremely difficult, if not impossible, to jam satellite broadcasts; any attempt by one country to do so would result in an act of space piracy, or a global telecommunications nuisance which the rest of the world could not permit.

It seems that we have, in the communications satellite, a technical device that may help to enforce good behaviour and cooperation even upon reluctant parties. (The meteorological satellite, with which it is closely linked, will do the same.) Its influence will be like that of air transport, though on a much larger scale and affecting whole nations rather than a relatively few favoured individuals. The inexorable force of astronomical facts will destroy the political fantasies which have so long fragmented our planet. For when all major artistic productions, entertainments, political and news events can be viewed simultaneously by the whole world, the parochialism and xenophobia of the past will be unable to survive.

This will be one major influence of communications satellites; another, perhaps even more fundamental, may be the reverse of a historic trend which has proceeded with scarcely a break for five thousand years. The traditional role of the city as a meeting place is coming to end; Megapolis may soon go the way of the dinosaurs it now resembles in so many respects. This century may see the beginnings of a slow but irresistible dispersion and decentralisation of mankind – a physical dispersion which will take place, paradoxically enough, at the same time as a cultural unification.

It will be none too soon, for it has been truly said that the measure of man's unhappiness is his estrangement from Nature. There is ample proof of this, in the fact that the most vicious of all savages are now to be found in the rotting stone jungles of our great cities. Civilization, in historic fact as well as in etymology, was the child of the city; but now it has outgrown its parent and must escape from its suffocating embrace.

It will be able to do so, when almost all the sense impressions, skills and facilities that we employ in everyday life become amenable to telecommunications – as they will. For, as I concluded in my address to the XIIth International Astronautical Congress in Washington, 1961:

> What we are building now is the nervous system of mankind. The communications network, of which the satellites will he nodal points, will enable the consciousness of our grandchildren to flicker like lightning back and forth across the face of this planet. They will be able to go anywhere and meet anyone, at any time, without stirring from their homes... all the museums and libraries of the world will be extensions of their living rooms.

And it will not matter where those living rooms may be; for on this planet, at least, the conquest of space will be complete. ❏

Sir Arthur C Clarke first developed the mathematical and engineering principles behind the comsat in a 1945 Wireless World *paper. This extract is taken from* Voices from the sky, *1965.* ©*Arthur C Clarke*

Afterword: In late 1998 the Iridium low-orbit network became operational, allowing direct satellite telephony from small, cheap handsets. Within eight years, another five networks of low orbit satellites are planned, allowing amongst other things high-bandwidth data communication to and from any part of the earth. Current trends suggest we will have high speed internet connection via a sub-$50 satellite handset/modem within ten years, giving cheap WWW access without expensive, ground-based phone networks. From the poles to the rainforest, the age of the truly public library will soon be here.
FF

MICHAEL FOLEY

A tale of three cities

New ideas concerning the role and purpose of journalism have provoked debate throughout the former Soviet Union, and more than a little confusion

There is a monument outside Moscow's Central House of Journalists depicting a Soviet journalist wearing a fine military uniform, high boots and a cape. He has a camera slung from his neck and holds a notebook with pencil poised. It is dedicated to all the journalists who covered the Great Patriotic War.

The journalist looks confidently ahead as the snow settles on his notebook, military cap and fine moustache. His role is to bring honour and glory to the Motherland and the Communist Party. Today few journalists are certain of a wage let alone a statue. Even the restaurant at the Central House of Journalists, formerly a meeting place for writers and journalists, has been contracted out. Few members of the Union could, in any case, afford to eat in it now.

None of this gloom is enough to stop a celebration though and the Russian Union of Journalists recently organised a conference and a whole number of receptions to celebrate its eightieth anniversary.

Over 200 delegates from journalists' unions from the length and breadth of Russia, as well as from central Asia, Ukraine, Belarus and the Baltic countries were at the House of Journalists. They came from Tajikistan, Turkmenistan and Uzbekistan, Armenia, Azerbaijan, Georgia. They included the young journalists' associations, the bodies that have sprung up to represent journalists working in the new and small independent media and to fight for press freedom.

The leaders of the old unions are survivors. Some were members of

The Hero Journalist – Credit: Novosti

the old Communist Party; in its new incarnation, the same Party that is now calling for tighter control of the media. The older among them are clearly nostalgic for the time when they were certain of their role and of a good income at the end of the week. Now they call for press freedom and freedom of expression and are linked to international organisations that were on the other side during the Cold War. At one of the many receptions a few old journos, after a number of vodkas, started to sing softly the old Soviet National Anthem. Gradually the sound increased. The little band that had been playing dance tunes joined in hesitantly at first, until more and more people started to stand up. Some of the younger delegates looked edgy and embarrassed as they saw that foreign guests had just recognised the tune. 'It's just old men remembering,' said one.

But while the leadership was celebrating the survival of its Union, even if as a shadow of its former Soviet self – the membership is about half what is was – there was little else for the media to celebrate. Seven years after the dissolution of the Soviet Union, there is still little press freedom. From Kazakhstan to Kyrgyzstan and Tajikistan to Belarus and Ukraine, the story is a dismal one: tax laws are used to harass financially; there is a growing body of laws forbidding insults of those in high places as well as of the president; compulsory registration of the media is common. Speaker after speaker accounted for the appalling state of press freedom in their countries. It was like that old comedy routine where two men compare the poverty of their youth: 'You think living in a cardboard box was bad. We couldn't even afford a box.'

And just to show that elections, or what usually passes for elections in this part of the world, are bad for journalists, several journalists with state-run news agencies in Kazakhstan reported to Human Rights Watch that they were explicitly warned against submitting stories even obliquely critical of President Nursultan Nazarbaev in the campaign leading up to the 10 January elections.

Back in Moscow, the Russian Union held a ceremony one evening where the union's president, Vsevolod Bogdanov, presented commemorative medals to the children of journalists who had died while reporting, a reminder that journalism is still a dangerous career option in Russia.

Meanwhile, in Kiev, a journalist attending a reception at a US diplomat's apartment, casually says that he has been fined US$1 million by the state. His newspaper is operating without telephones and has had to vacate its newsroom. He is not worried: US$500 would have worried him; that he would have had to pay. The harassment of his newspaper means he has not been paid for six months. Thankfully for him his wife has a job.

He and a few other Ukrainian journalists have been invited so that a US visitor can be apprised of the state of press freedom. The Ukrainians

present seem amused at this interest in their media. I cannot help
wondering if they are thinking of the US media and the
Clinton/Lewinsky coverage and pondering just how much they have to
learn about a free and independent press.

Kiev is a wonderful old city. Its stuccoed pastel coloured buildings
glow in the harsh light reflected by the snow. The opera house is
magnificent and the audience at the ballet reacts to the dance the way
fans of football do in other cultures, cheering and shouting approval for a
particular piece or movement. It is also the Wild West. A driver taking a
group to the airport was not being stopped by the many militia along
the road as was everyone else. 'My car is a good big car. They think I
might be Mafia,' he says. The driver, who looks about 16 years old,
produces a police identification. If they do stop the car he has no
intention of handing over the customary bribe. He will simply show his
identification.

'But no one will believe you are a policeman?'

'No, but they don't know who gave me the ID,' he grins. He has
masses of other identification as well, including a card that gives access to
the Parliament.

The main school of journalism in Ukraine is the Institute of
Journalism at the Kiev Taras Shevchenko University. It is housed in the
impressive if Stalinist former Communist Party School. The place is like
no other university anywhere. No graffiti. None at all. The females wear
skirts and the males ties. There are no books to be seen. None of the
piles of books and papers that occupy desks and shelves in other
universities. Discussion is similarly tidy. At a seminar organised as part of
an EU programme to aid journalists, academics and journalists read
paper after paper. Any questions were responded to with the comment
that the question was interesting and would be dealt with later. Later
never came.

Outside the warmth of the institute, ordinary journalists take two or
more jobs just to survive. Militia were taking money; flash foreign cars
drove Mafia through the city. With elections looming, there is a view
among human rights groups and journalists that press freedom is getting
worse and that President Leonid Kuchma is moving closer to that
ground now occupied by President Aleksandr Lukashenka of
neighbouring Belarus.

Journalists working in Minsk, the Belarus capital, fare worse than in any of the former Soviet republics. The former collective farm manager, now president, is almost universally shunned, and cannot even get membership of the Council of Europe, a body that is willing to embrace Turkey, Croatia and Ukraine. Independent newspapers are continually harassed and the biggest, *Svoboda*, has to be printed in Vilnius, across the border in Lithuania.

There is little or no investment in the independent press. Only one per cent of the economy is in the private sector and, in 1997, total foreign investment was only US$40 million. The electronic media is almost totally state-owned and the print media is forced to use state-owned printing plants where it is at the mercy of the authorities, as it is in its dealings with the state-run distribution system.

Sometimes one is left with the impression that Lukashenko is playing with the press. There is no doubt he could simply close it down completely if he chose; he prefers, instead, simply to make its life a misery.

The most recent case of harassment was of the Belarusian-language newspaper *Nasha Niva* which was warned that it had violated the Laws on Press and Other Mass Media for deviating from the accepted form of spelling and punctuation. The newspaper was using a form of spelling common in the 1920s until banned by Stalin. The Supreme Court ruled, on this occasion, in favour of the newspaper, but the chairman of the Committee on the Press, Mikhail Padgainy, has already filed a complaint and a request that the court revoke its own decision

Minsk has had a bad press. One old joke goes that you could build a wall round Minsk, call it Stalinland and people would pay to go into it as though it were a theme park. Some are convinced that it is the model for Malcolm Bradbury's take-off of all those East European travel guides that used to extol the beauty of the tractor factory: 'Welcome to Slaka'.

In fairness to the residents of Minsk, once Stalin had decided to reward them for their heroism in World War II by demolishing the old city, ancient urban heart of Europe's jewry, and replacing it with a model 1950s neo-brutal 'Hero Town', they were not given much choice as to their surroundings. It is probably the least unreconstructed part of the former USSR. Lenin looms down from plinths in the Metro and even the KGB has never felt it necessary to change its name. Its pale yellow stone Soviet neo-classical building stands impressively within a few blocks of a McDonalds.

Despite President Lukashenka, the poverty of those begging in the underpasses, the ubiquitous camouflage-wearing militia, I cannot help having a soft spot for Minsk. It might be a minority taste, but I like the way the river meanders through the city, its many parks, the old Soviet architectural grandeur and, above all, the friendliness of the people.

It is a city of policemen, who are everywhere in camouflage outfits, as if ready for a guerrilla war. They stop cars for spot checks and blow whistles if you attempt to cross one of the vast boulevards – wide enough to land a Boeing 747 they seem – without using the underpasses.

Meanwhile, back in Russia, the economic crisis has hit journalists in different ways. Regional newspapers have had to withdraw Moscow correspondents because of the costs. Some say this has placed them even more firmly under the thumb of the local authorities. Journalists are also increasingly willing to write complimentary pieces about local politicians or business interests in return for a fee. 'It's easy to be ethical when you're paid a wage,' one told me when we Western journalists expressed horror at this.

There has, however, been one unexpected benefit from the economic crisis. Alexei Simonov of the Glasnost Defence Foundation which monitors media abuses and provides legal help, says that the economic crisis forced the media to be less obsessed with themselves. They began to understand that survival was not just a media problem but one that concerned the whole of society; and that outside the power structures there was a society waiting to be addressed. Newspapers started to write 'how to survive' stories and have become more relevant. The number of newspapers has fallen, but total sales have increased. For the first time since the end of the Soviet Union, people are buying newspapers because they are useful and important to their lives.

The 'least bad situation' is in Russia, Kyrgyzstan and Moldova, says Simonov. It is getting worse in Ukraine which, like Kazakhstan, appears to be closing media ranks with Belarus. Turkmenistan, he adds, is the very worst case: 'There is no problem with freedom of speech in Turkmenistan because there is no such thing.' In Armenia there is a free press, of sorts, but there are no laws; In Azerbaijan, as in Belarus, there is one-man rule and little room for press freedom. ❑

Michael Foley is a media commentator at the Irish Times *and a lecturer in journalism at the Dublin Institute of Technology*

ARIF AZAD

Musical obsession

Pakistan has banned its most successful pop group ever - the prime minister doesn't like the lyrics or the tunes

Late last year, hard on the heels of its return from a sell-out tour of India, Pakistan's Council of the Arts ordered a probe into the activities of the country's leading pop group. In a letter headed 'Indian Subversive Propaganda', *Junoon* (Obsession) - number one among Pakistani and Indian youth abroad as well as at home - was accused of seeking to 'belittle the concept of the ideology of Pakistan', disagreeing with 'national opinion on nuclear tests', talking of 'cultural similarities' and hoping for 'the reunification of India and Pakistan'.

It was not the band's first brush with authority. It first attracted the hostility of Pakistan's political establishment in 1996 when its hit song *Ehtassab* (Accountability), lambasting corrupt politicians, was ordered off the airwaves on the grounds that it could destabilise the country before elections. The video included a scene of a horse dining at a five star hotel - a swipe at polo-loving husband of ex-Prime Minister Benazir Bhutto. Since then, official disfavour and overwhelming popular approval have gone hand in hand. The group's 1997 album *Azadi* (Freedom) boosted the band's appeal still further in Pakistan as well as across the border in India. '*Sayonee*' (Friends), the hit number on the album, became the best selling single in both countries. In Pakistan, however, it also brought *Junoon* into conflict with the country's powerful religious lobbies. The video of '*Sayonee*', shot on location at shrines in the historic city of Multan, led to accusations of 'belittling shrines' and 'bringing mysticism into disrepute' by pious religious zealots.

And there was more to follow. On Independence Day (14 August) 1997, the ruling Muslim League claimed the group's rendering of national poet Mohammed Iqbal's famous poem '*Khudi*' (Self-awareness)

Junoon – Credit: Junoon

was 'an insult to Iqbal'. The official reason advanced was that the group had exceeded its poetic license by garbling a number of disparate verses into a single song; in truth, the government did not look kindly on the renegade group's 'appropriation' of a poet – in his day also seen as a bit of a firebrand revolutionary – the establishment has come to claim as its own.

1997 ended with Pakistan's Prime Minister Nawaz Sharif banning all pop music from national television following a live performance on PTV (Pakistan Television): henceforth, he decreed, youngsters in jeans and with long hair – a dig at a new generation born out of globalised western musical culture – would not be tolerated on the national airwaves. His personal decision to impose the ban had two aims in mind: to put an end to the growing taste for politically charged pop music that was challenging his government's authority and, in the process, finally to see off his particular *bête noir*, the most popular politically engaged band of them all, *Junoon*.

Pakistan's problems with western-influenced pop music go back to the time of military dictator General Zia ul-Haq (1977-1988). Throughout his rule, he made strenuous efforts to control the musical agenda by promoting religious and apolitical music. This had limited appeal and groups like *Junoon* evolved in opposition to government efforts to impose a uniform and anodyne musical straightjacket on the country.

The band's popularity is based on its electic mix of musical traditions, a fusion of Sufi poetry inspired by Pakistan's greatest singer of traditional mystical music, Nusrat Fatheh Ali Khan, subcontinental folk, classical rhythms and western rock. The blend of Sufi poetry and mysticism – which recognises no borders and preaches syncretic religion – with western music is anathema to the right-wing conservative Pakistani establishment that, under pressure from the increasingly influential religious extremists, is demonstrating considerable sympathy for a Taliban-style social order in Pakistan. *Junoon's* composition testifies to the group's belief in diversity rather than the social and cultural isolation this implies: it is made up of lead singer Ali Azmat, songwriter and guitarist Salman Ahmad and US bass player Brian Thomas O'Connell.

Then came the trip to India. In March 1998, *Junoon* was invited to India to sing at the ZEE-TV Cine Award ceremony . The visit was a huge success and was followed by a concert tour across the country. The band's appearances attracted huge crowds of self-styled *Junoonis*; the Indian media lionised the group. As if this were not enough to sound alarm bells in high places back in Pakistan, India chose the moment of a packed *Junoon* concert in Chandigarh to detonate a nuclear device. The youthful crowd took up the cry of 'cultural fusion not nuclear fusion'.

Which was more than enough to justify the government's heavy-handed investigation and threats of the loss of citizenship on the group's return home. 'All we have done is denounce the concept of an arms race,' says Salman Ahmad. 'In Pakistan we don't have clean water, health or employment. How can we afford a nuclear race?'

While the ban on most pop groups has been lifted, *Junoon* remains off limits. According to Sheryar Ahmed, manager of the group, the official reason is that *Junoon* has exceeded the mandate of a pop group by embracing political themes in its songs. The group is currently producing a documentary on the history of its resistance to official censorship in Pakistan. ❑

Arif Azad was a reporter with the Pakistani magazine Viewpoint. *He now monitors South Asia for* Index

Further music censorship news:

●　**Ban for Linda:** 'You say I'm simple/you say I'm a hick/You're fucking no one/you stupid dick. These lines from Linda McCartney's 'The Light Comes From Within' have led to an alleged ban on her posthumous single by many of Britain's radio stations. Her husband, Sir Paul McCartney, published apparently tongue-in-cheek advertisements in the press defending the single and asking parents to use 'wisdom and good sense' in this 'vital matter'. But veteran Radio 1 DJ John Peel said that if such a ban existed it was more likely to be because the record was 'crap' rather than anything more sinister. ❏ *Martin Cloonan*

●　**'Sex On the Beach'**, a song by the Dutch-American group T-Spoon, has gone off the air in the Fiji Islands. Under pressure from the Fiji Islands assistant minister for information Ratu Josefa Dimuri, and criticism from religious and community leaders, Radio FM96 finally gave up the fight. On 16 January, it announced it was no longer playing the song despite the fact that it was the most requested number on the station. General manager Ian Jackson said, 'Our main purpose is to entertain people. If we offend people, then we will take it off the air.' But he added, 'Considering the issues this country faces, I was surprised to see the amount of publicity a song generated.' Jackson said the song was on the air for six weeks before someone complained to the government and that the station had received only four complaints, including one from the ministry of information.

FM96 is one of three popular stations owned by Communications Fiji Limited. It operates from Suva, the Fiji Islands capital, and is aimed at a 'young, modern market'. In a letter to Communications Fiji Limited, Dimuri reminded the company it had agreed to 'plan and present its programmes in a manner that respects the multi-cultural and multi-racial nature of Fiji society and will use its best endeavours to ensure that no offence is caused to the cultures, religions or morals of Fiji residents'. Fiji's Daily Post reported Dimuri as saying, I am very disappointed with the lack of moral decency in that particular radio station. We are working on the media review that will cover new broadcasting laws and that will deal with the content and quality of programmes that will be aired by radio stations in Fiji.' ❏
PINA Pacific Freedom of Information Network

Libraries & Culture

EDITOR: Donald G. Davis, Jr., University of Texas at Austin

Libraries & Culture is an interdisciplinary journal that explores the significance of collections of recorded knowledge — their creation, organization, preservation, and utilization — in the context of cultural and social history, unlimited as to time and place. Many articles deal with North American topics, but **L & C** also publishes articles on library history in other countries, as well as topics dealing with ancient and medieval libraries.

"Topics are diverse...Book reviews are detailed, evaluative, and scholarly in approach. This is a delightful journal, beautifully illustrated."
— **Magazines for Libraries 1995**

SPRING 1999, VOL. 34:2

Autonomy and Accomodation: Houston's
Colored Carnegie Library, 1907-1922
Cheryl Knott Malone

"The Greatest Morale Factor Next to the Red Army": Books and Libraries in
American and British Prisoners of War Camps in Germany during World War II
David Shavitt

Patricia Spereman and the Beginning of Work with
Children in Canadian Public Libraries
Lynne E. F. McKechnie

Unpacking: Walter Benjamin and His Library
Joseph D. Lewandowski

The Igbo in Diaspora: The Binding Force of Information
Amusi Odi

Single copy rates: Individual $14, Institution $22,
Canada/Mexico, add $2.50; other foreign, add $5 (airmail).
Yearly subscription rates: Individual $30, Institution $54,
Student/Retired $18,
Canada/Mexico, add $10; other foreign, add $20 (airmail).
Refunds available only on unshipped quantities of current subscriptions.

University of Texas Press Journals
Box 7819, Austin, Texas 78713-7819
Phone # 512-471-4531, Fax # 512-320-0668, journals@uts.cc.utexas.edu

BRIAN MCGEE

A skewed utopia

Cuba's National Library is not quite what it seems: mysteriously absent titles and a surfeit of exemplary works by the leader reflect the anxieties of the revolution

Kant, Diderot, Comte, Darwin, Descartes, Bacon, Aristotle, Plato. The founding fathers of modern thought, their names engraved in marble, adorn the façade of the *Biblioteca Nacional José Marti* in Havana. The main entrance honours local heroes, among them the writers Gertrudis de Avellaneda, José-Maria Heredia and Cyrillo Villaverde.

Inside, the lofty public reading room, with its imposing oak tables, high ceilings and a cooling breeze coming through its myriad windows, has hardly a seat to spare; studious readers of all ages pore over books and newspapers. It's a favourite place with many of Havana's students and as one of them put it, 'When I come here it always feels like I enter another reality, completely different from the world outside.'

So far, the *Biblioteca Nacional* seems no different from many others the world over. Yet users accustomed to libraries elsewhere might well experience browsing withdrawal symptoms. Access to books in the permanent collection is via a chit sent skywards to the gargantuan store rooms, the requested item appearing some minutes later. Only one book at a time may then be borrowed for two weeks; a further title may only be secured on the return of the first. Members of the Club Minerva, a private lending library costing 10 pesos (US$0.5) a year, have access to other books, including more recent foreign titles such as, for instance, Umberto Eco's *Foucault's Pendulum*.

Browsers are not completely frustrated, however: the reading room's reference section speaks volumes. While many of the foreign encyclopaedias date from the 1960s and 70s, the *Historia de España* series was published as recently as 1990. A whole series of Russian encyclopaedias, forlorn and dusty, ends abruptly in 1990, the year before the Soviet withdrawal from Cuba; a monumental 42-volume 1958 Buenos Aires edition of the complete works of Lenin in Spanish rests alongside looking equally neglected. For the courageous, there is also the *Libro de Cuba*, a gargantuan 1,000-page encyclopaedia published to mark the fiftieth anniversary of independence in 1902 and the centenary of the birth of José Marti, the journalist and Cuban national hero who died fighting the Spanish in 1895.

While there is certainly no shortage of the written word in Cuba, where the latest UN Human Development Report notes a 96 per cent literacy rate, the landscape changes shape once the index begins to divulge its secrets. The National Library's catalogue – in the process of computerisation – is contained in an immense series of cards that map the access to over 2.5 million items. The reader interested in freedom of expression finds only a modest 16 titles, including Fidel Castro's 1961 *Palabras a los intelectuales* and the1980 Havana-published *En Colombia no hay libertad de expresión*. There are no titles on Cuba, where six national journalists working for independent news agencies were arrested in a 10-day period in January this year. One of them, according to the Madrid daily *El País*, was sentenced to four years' imprisonment for 'dangerous social conduct'.

As for censorship itself, there are 13 titles relating to Britain, Mexico, Russia and Portugal, together with a 1959 South African title *Censorship and libraries*. In a country where all the publishing houses are state run, *el líder máximo* Fidel Castro said in 1971, 'There are some books of which we must publish not even one copy, not even one chapter, not even one page, not even one letter!' And while Cuba's difficult economic situation, in the context of the US trade embargo, is certainly a factor limiting the purchase of books, many writers in exile, such as Zoë Valdes, are effectively banned in their homeland.

In contrast, references to speeches and texts by Fidel Castro and his brother Raúl, head of the armed forces, are in plentiful supply: almost three entire card drawers, comprising hundreds upon hundreds of references, are available at the National Library. In a provincial town, some 17 copies of the book *Fidel y la Religión: conversaciones con Frei Betto* are available to borrowers. And on the cover of a 1998 edition of *La Revista del Libro Cubano*, a young Fidel is pictured reading.

Do books critical of the revolution have their place on Cuban library shelves? An extremely sensitive question for Cubans, even when asked in the most diplomatic and roundabout way possible, far away from potential eavesdroppers. Criticism is of course possible as long as it is serious and respectful, came the cautious reply from one librarian. As a former university professor now resident overseas explained, the most secure way of proffering the gentlest of criticism, even when it is not set down in print, is to quote an untouchable author such as Lenin or Marx. Especially if that criticism is in a university auditorium, where any unorthodox comments by teaching staff will not go unnoticed.

Still at the National Library, down in the reference section, a series of mysterious green lines, ruled across various titles in the catalogue, make their appearance. They denote books absent from this library's shelves. Explanations from library staff vary: they could be lent to other libraries, they perhaps never reached Havana after their circuitous route through five or six other countries. Either or both explanations are plausible, yet a sceptic might try to establish some connection between the titles. Would Shelley's 'Prometheus Unbound' be shunned because it speaks of liberation? And why are Ezra Pound's *Complete Cantos* missing from these shelves? More conclusively, every single Mario Vargas Llosa title is greenlined: despite the Peruvian-born writer's initial 'unconditional adhesion' to Cuba, he fell from grace in the regime's eyes in 1971.

The National Library is by no means the only storehouse of the written word in Cuba. In Havana alone there is a whole range of libraries, among them the *Casa de las Américas*, a cultural centre renowned for its Latin-American literary festivals, the National Archive and the Library of the Institute of Literature and Linguistics. In fact there are over 5,000 school, 60 university and 300 specialised libraries spread over the length and breadth of the island. In all of them books, both by their presence and their absence, together with their readers, give us part of the picture of what the Argentinian-born writer Alberto Manguel has called 'Cuba's skewed utopia'. ❏

Brian McGee is a graduate student based in Montreal, Canada

Support for

INDEX

Index thanks
The Norwegian Royal Ministry of Foreign Affairs
for their support of *Word Power*

Index on Censorship and the *Writers and Scholars Educational Trust (WSET)* were founded to protect and promote freedom of expression. The work of maintaining and extending freedoms never stops. Freedom of expression is not self-perpetuating but has to be maintained by constant vigilance.

The work of *Index* and *WSET* is only made possible thanks to the generosity and support of our many friends and subscribers world-wide. We depend on donations to guarantee our independence; to fund research and to support projects which promote free expression.

The Trustees and Directors would like to thank the many individuals and organisations who support *Index on Censorship* and Writers and Scholars Educational Trust, including:

Anonymous
The Ajahma Charitable Trust
The Arts Council of England
The Bromley Trust
The John S Cohen Foundation
Danish International Development Agency (DANIDA)
Demokratifonden
The European Commission
The Ford Foundation
Fritt Ord Foundation
The Goldbergh Family Trust
The Golsonscott Foundation
The JM Kaplan Fund
The Lyndhurst Settlement
Neda

The Open Society Institute
The Onaway Trust
Pearson plc Charitable Trust
The Prins Claus Trust
The Ruben and Elisabeth Rausing Trust
CA Rodewald Charitable Settlemet
EJB Rose Charitable
The Royal Literary Fund
The Alan and Babette Sainsbury Charitable Fund
Scottish Media Group plc
Stephen Spender Memorial Fund
Tom Stoppard
Swedish International Development Co-operation Agency
United News and Media plc
UNESCO

If you would like more information about *Index on Censorship* or would like to support our work, please contact Hugo Grieve, Fundraising Manager, on (44) 171 278 2313 or e-mail hugo@indexoncensorship.org